SCHOLASTIC

AF650331

Exploring Social Studies 5

Name ______________________________

Class ______________________________

Photo credits and attributions:

p. 10: http://commons.wikimedia.org/wiki/File:Goliath_Frog.jpg by Ryan Somna; Fables; p. 38: http://commons.wikimedia.org/wiki/File:South_American_jungle_photograph.jpg by Sascha Grabow; http://commons.wikimedia.org/wiki/File:Mile%C5%A1ovka_(837_m),_pohled_z_lesa_na_%C3%BApat%C3%AD.JPG by Juan de Vojníkov; p. 45: Fables; p. 46: Fables; p. 52: http://commons.wikimedia.org/wiki/File:Kalahari_PICT0036_.JPG by Winfried Bruenken (Amrum); http://commons.wikimedia.org/wiki/File:Desierto_Atacama.jpg by Christian Van Der Henst S.; http://commons.wikimedia.org/wiki/File:Pinnacles_Desert,_Western_Australia.jpg by Zoharby; http://commons.wikimedia.org/wiki/File:Sonora_Desert_2007.jpg by Tomas Castelazo; http://commons.wikimedia.org/wiki/File:Thar_desert_Rajasthan_India.jpg by Sushmita Balasubramani; p. 53: http://commons.wikimedia.org/wiki/File:Stenocereus_thurberi_North_Puerto_Blanco_Scenic_Drive_3.jpg by Ken Lund; http://commons.wikimedia.org/wiki/File:Calliandra_californica_3.jpg by Tatiana Gerus; http://commons.wikimedia.org/wiki/File:Green_ephedra_Ephedra_viridis_bush.jpg by Dcrjsr; p. 54: http://commons.wikimedia.org/wiki/File:Fennec_WhiteDesert.jpg by HelmutBoehm; Fables; p. 55: Fables; p. 56: http://commons.wikimedia.org/wiki/File:Bedouin.jpg by nbahan; p. 57: http://commons.wikimedia.org/wiki/File:Adelie_Penguins_diving,_Hope_Bay.jpg by Angell Williams; p. 58: http://commons.wikimedia.org/wiki/File:Eisb%C3%A4r_1996-07-23.jpg by Ansgar Walk; p. 63: Fables; p. 64: http://commons.wikimedia.org/wiki/File:Thomsons-gazelle.jpg by Erik A. Drabløs; http://commons.wikimedia.org/wiki/File:Topi_rwanda.jpg by Anne-Sophie Olbrechts; http://commons.wikimedia.org/wiki/File:Friendly_Female_Koala.JPG by Quartl; Fables; p. 65: Fables; p. 69: http://commons.wikimedia.org/wiki/File:Alaska.jpg by steve lyon; p. 70: http://commons.wikimedia.org/wiki/File:Antarctica_(7),_Laubeuf_Fjord,_Webb_Island.JPG by Vincent van Zeijst; p. 71: http://commons.wikimedia.org/wiki/File:Nunavut_tundra_-c.jpg by ADialla; p. 72: Fables; p. 77: http://commons.wikimedia.org/wiki/File:Homayouns_tomb_side_view_2006.JPG by Amir85; p. 78: http://commons.wikimedia.org/wiki/File:Khajuraho_Devi_Jagadambi_Temple_2010.jpg by Marcin Białek; http://commons.wikimedia.org/wiki/File:Shore_temple_04.jpg by KenWalker; http://commons.wikimedia.org/wiki/File:St_Paul%27s_Cathedral,_Kolkata.jpg by Mjanich ; p. 80: http://commons.wikimedia.org/wiki/File:Taj_Mahal_in_March_2004.jpg by Dhirad; p. 81: http://commons.wikimedia.org/wiki/File:Agra_Fort_14.JPG by Sanyambahga; p. 82: Fables; http://commons.wikimedia.org/wiki/File:Jama_Masjid,_Delhi,_morning_view.jpg by Dennis Jarvis; p. 83: http://commons.wikimedia.org/wiki/File:India_-_Madurai_temple_-_0781.jpg by Jorge Royan; Fables; p. 84: http://commons.wikimedia.org/wiki/File:Sanchi_Stupa.jpg by Marc Shandro; http://commons.wikimedia.org/wiki/File:Gateway_of_India.jpg by Rhaessner; p. 85: http://commons.wikimedia.org/wiki/File:Rock_painting,_Bhimbetka,_Raisen_district,_MP.jpg by Yann; p. 86: http://commons.wikimedia.org/wiki/File:Ellora,_maharashtra_1997015.jpg by Benjamín Preciado ; p. 106: http://commons.wikimedia.org/wiki/File:Charkha_kept_at_Gandhi_Ashram.jpg by Jigar Brahmbhatt; p. 109: http://commons.wikimedia.org/wiki/File:QUITIN7.JPG by Dore Chakravarty.

First edition 2012
Reprinted 2012, 2013, 2014 (thrice), 2018 (twice), 2019, 2020, 2022, 2023, 2025, 2026

ISBN 978-81-8477-939-4

Printed in India at Shiv Shakti Printing and Trading Co., Haryana

Contents

Introduction 4

1. Continents and Oceans 6
2. Latitudes and Longitudes 19
3. Movements of the Earth 27
4. The Temperature Zones 35
5. The Equatorial Forests 41
6. The Deserts 50
7. The Temperate Zone 61
8. The Frigid Zone 68
9. Indian Heritage and Culture 76
10. The Advent of the British Raj 89
11. The First Battle for Independence 95
12. The Struggle towards Complete Independence 104
13. Our Leaders 113
14. Religious and Social Reformers 121
15. Our Rights and Duties 129
16. The United Nations 135

How to Use an Atlas 142
How to Use an Encyclopedia 143
How to Use the Internet 144

 ISBN 978-81-8477-939-4

Introduction

Exploring Social Studies is an exciting social studies series for levels 1 to 5. The books have been designed to fulfill the requirements of the National Curriculum Framework (NCF), which has been adopted by CBSE, ICSE and major State Educational Boards.

The series adopts a learner-centred approach, encouraging students to make connections between their role in their immediate environment and the world around them. The coursebooks are filled with lots of colourful photographs, maps and illustrations that expose students to real-life everyday experiences from around the world.

In addition, the series prepares students to meet the challenges of the future by

- following pyramidal pedagogy
- encouraging exploration and innovation
- facilitating observation and logical analysis to support conclusions
- promoting independent learning

Learn More provides activities that hone the students' ability to absorb, infer, classify, experiment and predict.

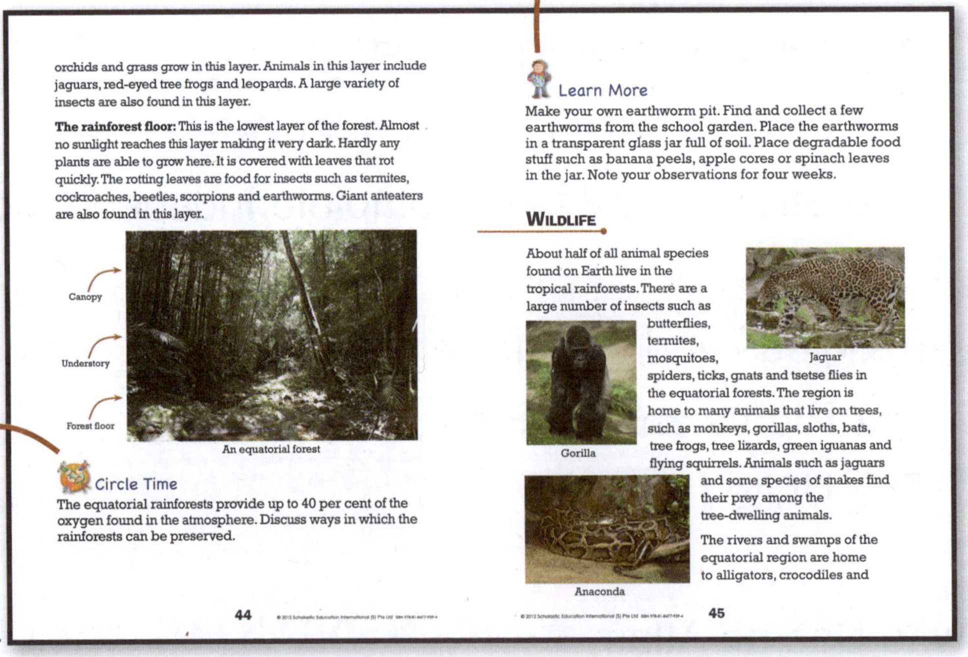

orchids and grass grow in this layer. Animals in this layer include jaguars, red-eyed tree frogs and leopards. A large variety of insects are also found in this layer.

The rainforest floor: This is the lowest layer of the forest. Almost no sunlight reaches this layer making it very dark. Hardly any plants are able to grow here. It is covered with leaves that rot quickly. The rotting leaves are food for insects such as termites, cockroaches, beetles, scorpions and earthworms. Giant anteaters are also found in this layer.

An equatorial forest

Circle Time

The equatorial rainforests provide up to 40 per cent of the oxygen found in the atmosphere. Discuss ways in which the rainforests can be preserved.

44

Learn More

Make your own earthworm pit. Find and collect a few earthworms from the school garden. Place the earthworms in a transparent glass jar full of soil. Place degradable food stuff such as banana peels, apple cores or spinach leaves in the jar. Note your observations for four weeks.

WILDLIFE

About half of all animal species found on Earth live in the tropical rainforests. There are a large number of insects such as butterflies, termites, mosquitoes, spiders, ticks, gnats and tsetse flies in the equatorial forests. The region is home to many animals that live on trees, such as monkeys, gorillas, sloths, bats, tree frogs, tree lizards, green iguanas and flying squirrels. Animals such as jaguars and some species of snakes find their prey among the tree-dwelling animals.

The rivers and swamps of the equatorial region are home to alligators, crocodiles and

Jaguar

Gorilla

Anaconda

45

Circle Time promotes exchange of ideas and techniques while laying emphasis on working as a team.

 ISBN 978-81-8477-939-4

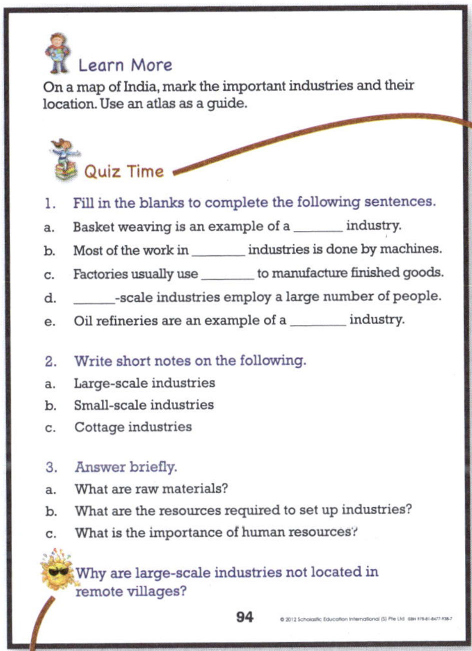

Learn More

On a map of India, mark the important industries and their location. Use an atlas as a guide.

Quiz Time

1. Fill in the blanks to complete the following sentences.
a. Basket weaving is an example of a _______ industry.
b. Most of the work in _______ industries is done by machines.
c. Factories usually use _______ to manufacture finished goods.
d. _______-scale industries employ a large number of people.
e. Oil refineries are an example of a _______ industry.

2. Write short notes on the following.
a. Large-scale industries
b. Small-scale industries
c. Cottage industries

3. Answer briefly.
a. What are raw materials?
b. What are the resources required to set up industries?
c. What is the importance of human resources?

Why are large-scale industries not located in remote villages?

94

Factastic imparts interesting information and facts related to the topic under discussion.

Quiz Time tests knowledge retention and serves as a quick recap of the lesson.

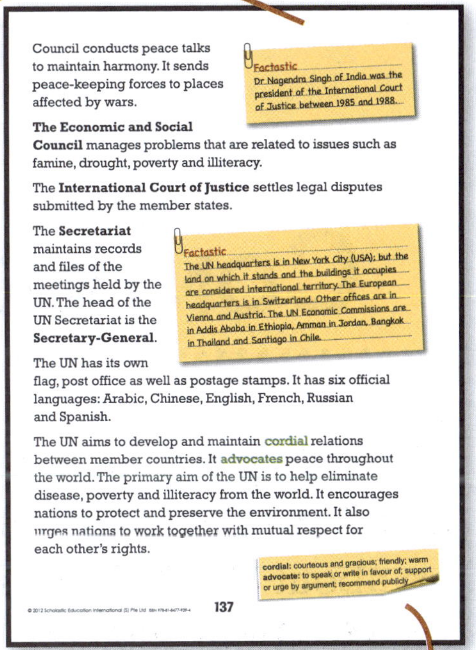

Council conducts peace talks to maintain harmony. It sends peace-keeping forces to places affected by wars.

Factastic
Dr Nagendra Singh of India was the president of the International Court of Justice between 1985 and 1988.

The Economic and Social Council manages problems that are related to issues such as famine, drought, poverty and illiteracy.

The **International Court of Justice** settles legal disputes submitted by the member states.

The **Secretariat** maintains records and files of the meetings held by the UN. The head of the UN Secretariat is the **Secretary-General.**

Factastic
The UN headquarters is in New York City (USA); but the land on which it stands and the buildings it occupies are considered international territory. The European headquarters is in Switzerland. Other offices are in Vienna and Austria. The UN Economic Commissions are in Addis Ababa in Ethiopia, Amman in Jordan, Bangkok in Thailand and Santiago in Chile.

The UN has its own flag, post office as well as postage stamps. It has six official languages: Arabic, Chinese, English, French, Russian and Spanish.

The UN aims to develop and maintain cordial relations between member countries. It advocates peace throughout the world. The primary aim of the UN is to help eliminate disease, poverty and illiteracy from the world. It encourages nations to protect and preserve the environment. It also urges nations to work together with mutual respect for each other's rights.

cordial: courteous and gracious; friendly; warm
advocate: to speak or write in favour of; support or urge by argument; recommend publicly

137

Higher Order Thinking Skills (HOTS) questions are included in levels 4 and 5. These questions sharpen the students' skills of making inferences, understanding the logic behind a concept and thinking outside the box.

New and difficult words are defined in the **glossary**.

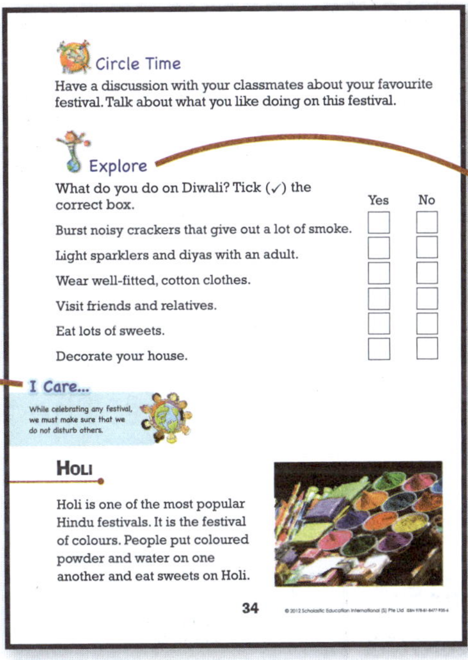

Circle Time

Have a discussion with your classmates about your favourite festival. Talk about what you like doing on this festival.

Explore

What do you do on Diwali? Tick (✓) the correct box.

	Yes	No
Burst noisy crackers that give out a lot of smoke.	☐	☐
Light sparklers and diyas with an adult.	☐	☐
Wear well-fitted, cotton clothes.	☐	☐
Visit friends and relatives.	☐	☐
Eat lots of sweets.	☐	☐
Decorate your house.	☐	☐

I Care...

While celebrating any festival, we must make sure that we do not disturb others.

HOLI

Holi is one of the most popular Hindu festivals. It is the festival of colours. People put coloured powder and water on one another and eat sweets on Holi.

34

Explore encourages students to analyse and question.

I Care provides value education in levels 1 to 3.

Students are taught to use an atlas, an encyclopedia and the Internet in levels 3 to 5 to do basic research individually and in groups, to present reports and projects. These help build the student's ability to learn independently.

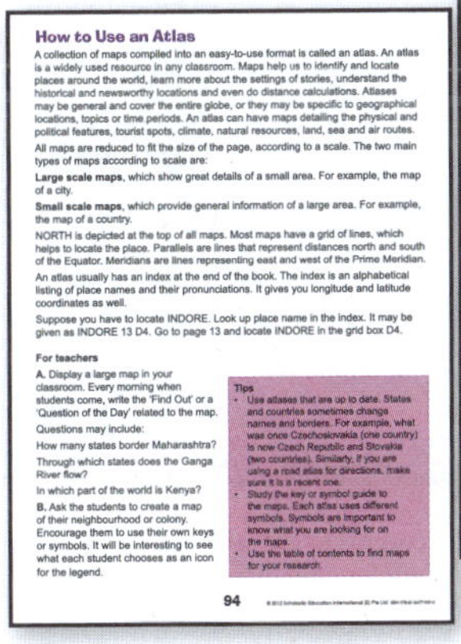

How to Use an Atlas

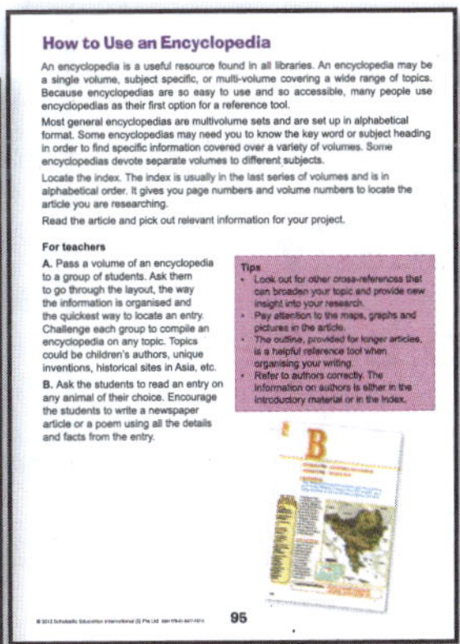

How to Use an Encyclopedia

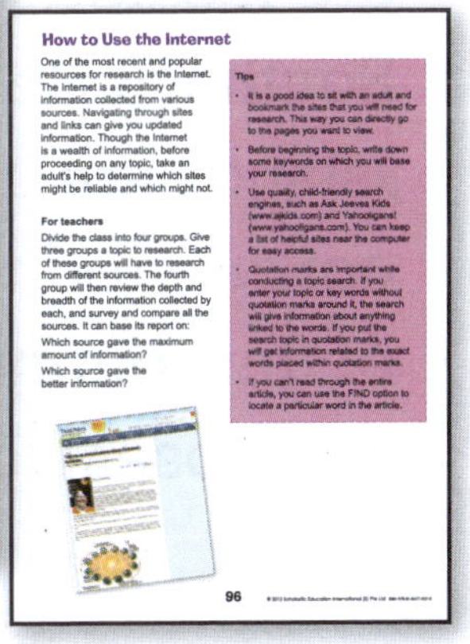

How to Use the Internet

1 CONTINENTS AND OCEANS

About 29 per cent of the Earth's surface is covered with land and 71 per cent by water. Oceans, seas, lakes and rivers make up about 361,000,000 square km, while the total land surface area is about 150,000,000 square km. The land surface has mountains, valleys, plains, forests and deserts.

Earth's land is divided into large land masses called continents. There are seven continents—Africa, Antarctica, Asia, Australia, Europe, North America and South America.

Two-thirds of the continental land mass is located in the Northern Hemisphere. Asia, Europe and North America are located in the Northern Hemisphere. The northern parts of Africa and South America also lie in the Northern Hemisphere. Australia and Antarctica are located in the Southern Hemisphere. Islands are usually considered to be part of the continent they are closest to.

Earth's continents

 ISBN 978-81-8477-939-4

The pie chart depicts the area covered by the continents in square km.

Land Area Covered by the Continents (in percentage)

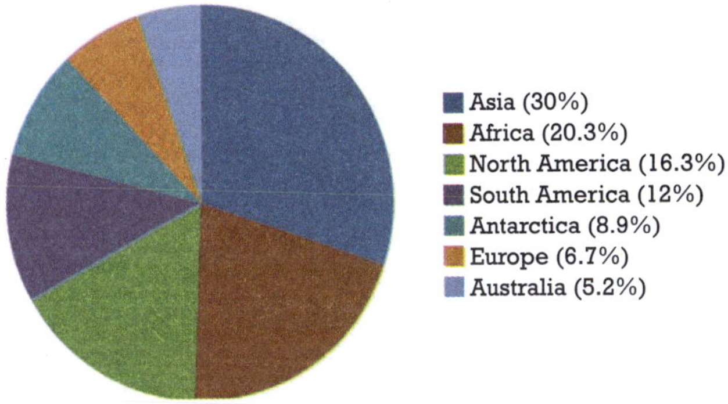

Factastic

About 200 million years ago, all continents were part of a single land mass known as Pangaea, which later broke up as a result of the continental drift. As these land masses moved away from each other, the seven continents emerged. This drift also resulted in the formation of mountains, mountain ranges, as well as the oceans and seas that we see today.

PERMIAN PERIOD

TRIASSIC PERIOD

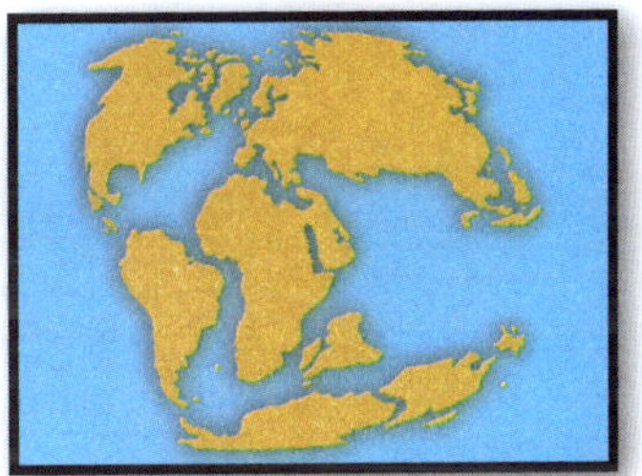
JURASSIC PERIOD

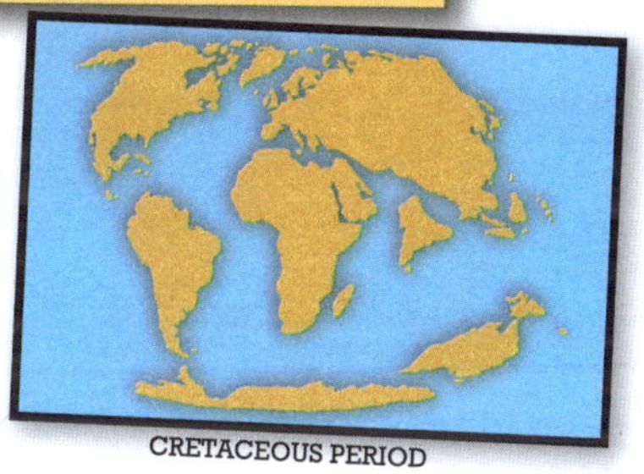
CRETACEOUS PERIOD

PRESENT DAY

Continents

Asia

Asia is the largest continent in the world. Europe and Asia are sometimes referred to as a single continent, **Eurasia**.

Asia is made up of forty-eight countries. It is surrounded by the Arctic Ocean to the north, the Indian Ocean to the south, the Pacific Ocean to the east and Europe to the west.

 ISBN 978-81-8477-939-4

Asia covers about 30 per cent of the Earth's land mass. Most of Asia lies in the Northern Hemisphere except for some Southeast Asian islands. Asia's coastline is longer than that of any other continent.

Asia

Asia is divided into West Asia, Central Asia, South Asia, East Asia, Southeast Asia and North Asia. India and her immediate neighbours are collectively known as the Indian **subcontinent**.

Asia is home to about 60 per cent of the human population. Nearly 4 billion people live in Asia. Seven out of ten of the most populated countries are in Asia. China is the world's most populated country. Some of the world's largest cities, such as Shanghai (China) and Mumbai (India) are located in Asia.

 ISBN 978-81-8477-939-4

The important rivers that flow through Asia include the Yangtze in China and the Ganga in India. The world's deepest lake, Lake Baikal, is in Asia.

Asia has a wide variety of plant and animal life. It is the only continent where tigers are found in the wild.

> **Factastic**
> The highest point in Asia is the summit of Mount Everest and the lowest point is on the shore of the Dead Sea.

AFRICA

Africa is the second-largest continent in the world. It is surrounded by the Mediterranean Sea to the north, the Atlantic Ocean to the west, the Indian Ocean and the Red Sea to the east.

Africa covers an area of about 30,365,000 square km. It covers about 20 per cent of the Earth's total land area.

Africa

Africa is the second most-populated continent on Earth. About 20 per cent of the world's population lives in Africa. There are more countries in Africa than in any other continent.

The Nile, the longest river in the world, and the Sahara Desert, the largest desert in the world, are in Africa.

The Suez Canal connects the Mediterranean Sea to the Red Sea.

 ISBN 978-81-8477-939-4

The world's biggest frog is found mainly in Cameroon (Africa). Named the Goliath frog, its body can be up to one foot long!

The African elephant is the largest living land animal.

Factastic

The African continent, once referred to by Europeans as the Dark Continent, is rich in mineral and natural resources. Most of the world's diamonds and gold come from Africa. Africa also has diverse wildlife and plant varieties.

Learn More

Look up an encyclopedia or the Internet to find out the main differences between African elephants and Asian elephants. Present your findings in a chart.

North America

North America is the third-largest continent in the world. It comprises Mexico, Canada and the United States of America as well as the countries of Central America and the Caribbean Islands. Canada is the largest country in the continent and the second-largest in the world.

The continent of North America is the only continent that lies completely in the northern and western hemispheres. North America is surrounded by the Arctic Ocean to the north, the Atlantic Ocean to the east, the Pacific Ocean to the west and the Caribbean Sea to the south.

 ISBN 978-81-8477-939-4

North America is very rich in minerals and other natural resources.

North America

The continent stretches from the frigid area of the Arctic Circle to the tropical rainforests of Central America. Lake Superior, located in the United States, is the world's largest freshwater lake with a surface area of about 82,100 square km. The Rocky Mountains stretch along the western part of the continent and the Appalachian Mountains stretch along the eastern part of the continent.

Factastic

The highest point in the North American continent is Mount McKinley in Alaska, which is 20,322 feet (6,194 m) tall. The lowest point is in the Badwater Basin in the Death Valley, California, which lies 282 feet (86 m) below sea level.

frigid: extremely cold

 ISBN 978-81-8477-939-4

South America

South America is the fourth–largest continent in the world. It is surrounded by the Caribbean Sea to the north, the Atlantic Ocean to the east, the Pacific Ocean to the west and Antarctica to the south. The Isthmus of Panama joins North America to South America.

South America

Explore

Find out what an isthmus is. Write a short paragraph on it and illustrate with a diagram. Locate a few isthmuses on a world map.

 ISBN 978-81-8477-939-4

South America has the largest rainforest on Earth, the Amazon Rainforest. It has the largest river by volume, the Amazon River. The world's longest mountain range, the Andes, is also in South America.

> **Factastic**
> The Atacama Desert is the driest place on Earth. It is located in Chile, in the continent of South America.

ANTARCTICA

Antarctica, the southernmost continent, is permanently covered with ice. It is also known as the White Continent. Antarctica is the coldest and windiest place on Earth.

Antarctica is the only continent that does not have a permanent human population. It has research stations where groups of scientists conduct studies. Thousands of tourists visit the continent every year.

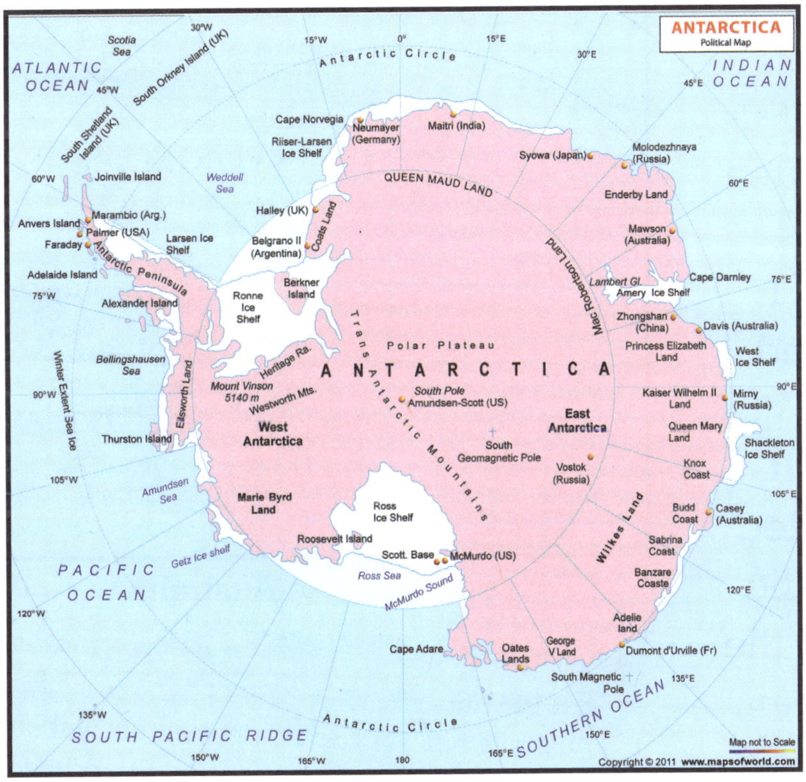

Antarctica

 ISBN 978-81-8477-939-4

EUROPE

Europe is the world's second-smallest continent. It is surrounded by the Arctic Ocean to the north, the Atlantic Ocean to the west, the Mediterranean Sea, the Black Sea and the Caspian Sea to the south. It is separated from Asia by the Ural Mountains and the Ural River.

Europe

AUSTRALIA

Australia is the smallest continent. It covers an area of 7,692,024 square km. It is also called the Island Continent. It is surrounded by the Pacific Ocean and the Indian Ocean.

Australia

Factastic

Australia has very sparse human population. It is the only continent in the world that has more sheep than people!

 ISBN 978-81-8477-939-4

Australia, New Zealand, Papua New Guinea and several atolls and islands of the South Pacific Ocean are collectively called **Australasia**.

The Great Barrier Reef, the largest reef system on Earth, is in Australia.

Circle Time

Divide your class into groups of four–five students. Each group should make a project on any one continent of their choice. The project must provide details of the location of the continent, its main countries, its main physical features and things that make it unique.

OCEANS

Oceans make up about 99 per cent of the Earth's living space. A vast variety of plant and animal life thrives in the oceans.

> **Factastic**
> The average depth of the oceans is 4 km. The Challenger Deep in the Mariana Trench in the Pacific Ocean is the deepest point on Earth. It lies at a depth of about 11 km.

There are five oceans on Earth. They are the Atlantic, Arctic, Indian, Pacific and Southern oceans.

Learn More

Find out the names and locations of any five seas and any five major lakes in the world. Mark them on a physical map of the world.

 ISBN 978-81-8477-939-4

Oceans of the world

Atlantic Ocean

The Atlantic Ocean is the second largest ocean. It lies between Africa, Europe and the Southern Ocean in the Western Hemisphere. It covers about 20 per cent of the Earth's surface. The deepest point in the Atlantic Ocean is the Puerto Rico Trench (about 8,380 m).

The Atlantic Ocean has several high peaks that form islands in it. The Mid-Atlantic Ridge is the longest continuous mountain range on Earth. It is about 16,000 km long.

Arctic Ocean

The Arctic Ocean is the smallest and shallowest ocean. It is located between Europe, Asia, and North America,

Factastic

The northernmost point of the Earth, the North Pole, is located in the middle of the Arctic Ocean. It remains frozen throughout the year.

 ISBN 978-81-8477-939-4

mostly north of the Arctic Circle. It covers an area of about 14,090,000 square km. The deepest point of the Arctic Ocean is in the Eurasian Basin.

Indian Ocean

The Indian Ocean is the third largest ocean. It lies between Africa, the Southern Ocean, Asia and Australia. It covers an area of about 73,440,000 square km. Its deepest point is the Java Trench at a depth of 7,450 m. It is the only ocean whose name originates from the name of a country—India.

Pacific Ocean

The Pacific Ocean is the largest ocean. It lies between the Southern Ocean, Asia, and Australia in the Western Hemisphere. It occupies about one-third of the Earth's surface. It covers an area of about 165,250,000 square km. The deepest point in the Pacific Ocean is the Mariana Trench at a depth of about 11 km.

Southern Ocean

The Southern Ocean (or the Antarctic Ocean) was recognised in the year 2000. The Southern Ocean is now recognised as the fourth largest of the world's five oceans.

Quiz Time

1. Name the following.

a. The world's biggest ocean

b. The fourth-largest continent in the world

 ISBN 978-81-8477-939-4

c. The smallest continent in the world

d. The deepest point in the ocean floor

e. The shallowest ocean in the world

2. On a physical map of the world, mark the following.

a. Antarctica

b. Indian Ocean

c. Africa

d. Southern Ocean

e. Australia

3. Fill in the blanks to complete the following sentences.

a. __________ is the biggest desert in the world.

b. __________ is the largest freshwater lake in the world.

c. There are _______ continents in the world.

d. __________ per cent of the Earth is covered by land.

e. The __________ of Panama joins North America to South America.

4. Answer the questions.

a. What is a continent?

b. Name the Earth's oceans.

c. What is Pangaea?

d. Which two continents share the same land mass?

Do you think oceans are important? Give reasons for your answer.

 ISBN 978-81-8477-939-4

2 Latitudes and Longitudes

The total surface area of the Earth is about 510 million square km. The land surface has countries, cities, towns and all other natural and man-made features.

Just like our houses have addresses that make it easy for us to locate them, geographers have designed imaginary lines that run horizontal and vertical and make it easy to locate places on the Earth's surface. These lines are known as **latitudes** and **longitudes**.

> Factastic
> The Earth is known as the 'Blue Planet' because, as observed from space, the atmosphere combined with the oceans makes the planet look blue in colour.

The Earth spins around on its axis. One end of the axis is the North Pole and the other is the South Pole. The **Equator** is an imaginary line that runs horizontally around the centre of the Earth. It is at an equal distance from both the poles.

Latitudes

Lines of latitude are imaginary lines that run horizontally across the Earth's centre. They are also called parallels because they run parallel to each other.

geographers: people who specialise in geographical research, explanation and study

 ISBN 978-81-8477-939-4

The 0° line of latitude is called the Equator. The Equator divides the Earth into two halves—the Northern Hemisphere and the Southern Hemisphere. The Equator is the starting point for measuring latitudes. The parallels of latitude help us measure the location of places north and south of the Equator.

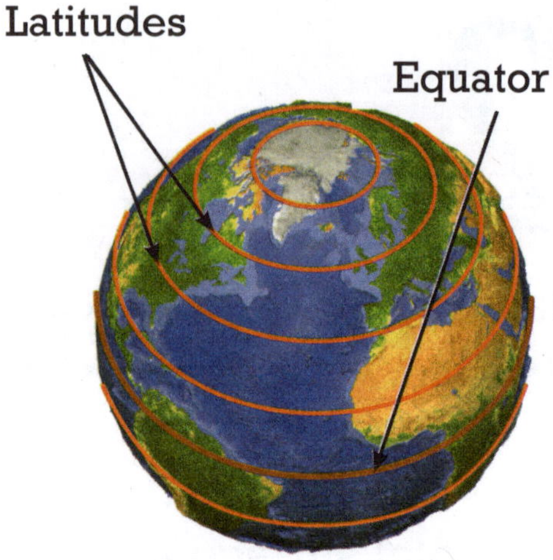

Earth's latitudes

The actual distance between parallels of latitude is always the same. Each parallel of latitude goes around the globe forming a circle. The Equator has the longest circumference. As we go closer to the poles, the circumference of the parallels of latitude gets smaller and smaller. The North Pole and the South Pole are just points.

Reading Latitude

Latitudes that lie north of the Equator are called north latitudes. Latitudes that lie south of the Equator are called south latitudes. The degree of each latitude is denoted by 'North' or 'South'. There are 90 degrees of latitude going north from the Equator. The North Pole is at 90° North. There are 90 degrees of latitude to the south of the Equator. The South Pole is at 90° South.

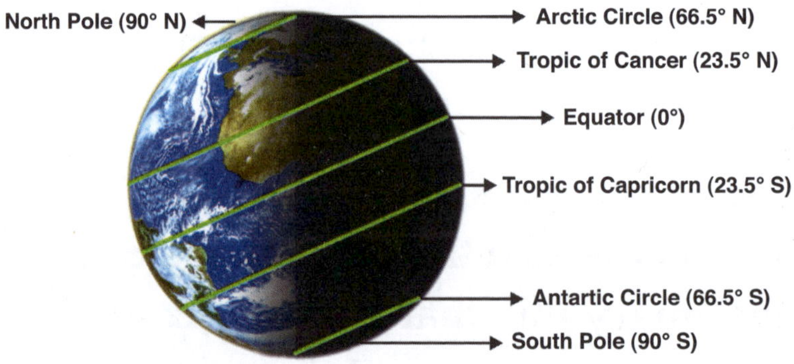

Earth's important latitudes

10° N is the latitude at 10 degrees in the Northern Hemisphere. Similarly, 10° S is the latitude at 10 degrees in the Southern Hemisphere.

 ISBN 978-81-8477-939-4

The 23.5° N latitude is known as the **Tropic of Cancer**. The 23.5° S latitude is known as the **Tropic of Capricorn**. The 66.5° N latitude is known as the **Arctic Circle**. The 66.5° S latitude is known as the **Antarctic Circle**. The Equator is the longest latitude at 0°.

Explore

Use an atlas and find the names of countries through which the Tropic of Capricorn passes.

Longitudes

Lines of longitude are imaginary lines that run parallel to the **Prime Meridian**. The Prime Meridian runs vertically from the North Pole to the South Pole. Lines of longitude are also called meridians. The Prime Meridian passes through Greenwich, near London. It is also known as the Greenwich Meridian.

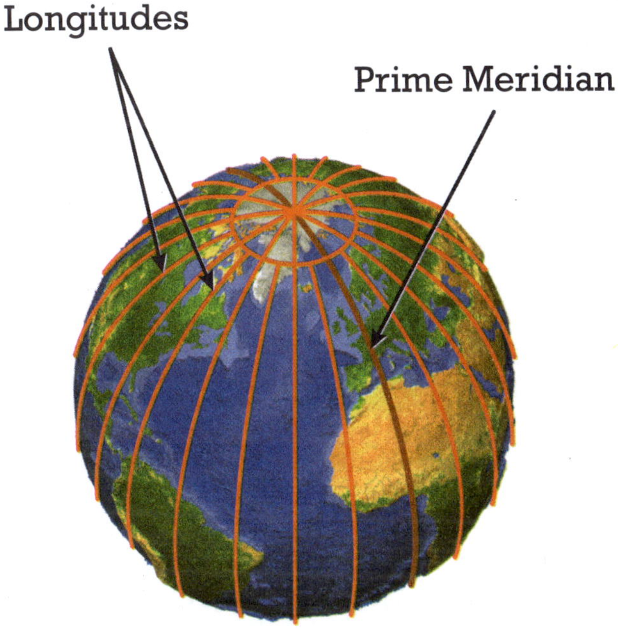

Earth's longitudes

The Prime Meridian divides the Earth into two halves—the Eastern Hemisphere and the Western Hemisphere. The Prime Meridian is the starting point for measuring longitudes. It has been given the value of 0 degrees of longitude. The meridians of longitude help us measure the location of places east and west of the Prime Meridian.

Meridians of longitude do not run parallel to one another.

 ISBN 978-81-8477-939-4

As we get closer to the poles, the distance between meridians decreases. All meridians of longitude meet at the poles. Meridians of longitude run perpendicular to parallels of latitude.

All meridians of longitude pass through both the poles. They are semicircles. The Earth is divided equally into 360 degrees of longitude. There are 180 degrees of longitude to the east of the Prime Meridian. There are also 180 degrees of longitude to the west of the Prime Meridian.

Reading Longitude

10° E is the longitude at 10 degrees in the Eastern Hemisphere. Similarly, 10° W is the longitude at 10 degrees in the Western Hemisphere.

> **Remember this!**
>
> The 180° E and 180° W longitudes are the same longitude. Similarly, the 0° and 360° longitudes are the same longitude.

Degrees of longitude have been divided into minutes (′) and seconds (″). There are 60 minutes in each degree. Each minute is divided into 60 seconds. These divisions help us calculate the location of a place accurately.

Latitude and Longitude Grid

When we combine parallels of latitude and meridians of longitude, we get a grid that covers the globe. Every point on the grid can be defined by a north/south degree and an east/west degree. This means that any place on Earth can be located if the latitude and the longitude are known.

 ISBN 978-81-8477-939-4

Explore

Use an atlas to find the latitude and longitude of the following cities.

City	Latitude	Longitude
Tokyo, Japan		
Beijing, China		
New Delhi, India		
Johannesburg, South Africa		
Moscow, Russian Federation		
London, United Kingdom		
New York, USA		
Rio de Janeiro, Brazil		

TIME

The meridians of longitude help us calculate the time of a particular place.

The Earth takes 24 hours to complete one rotation.

24 hours = 24 × 60 minutes = 1440 minutes

The Earth is divided into 360 meridians of longitude.

Therefore, 1440/360 = 4 minutes

This means that the Earth takes 4 minutes to rotate one degree, that is, the time difference between two consecutive meridians is 4 minutes.

 ISBN 978-81-8477-939-4

If the time at Greenwich (0°) is 12 am, then the time at 1° E will be 12.04 am and the time at 1° W will be 11.56 pm.

Therefore, if we know the time at Greenwich and the longitude of a place, we can calculate the local time of that place.

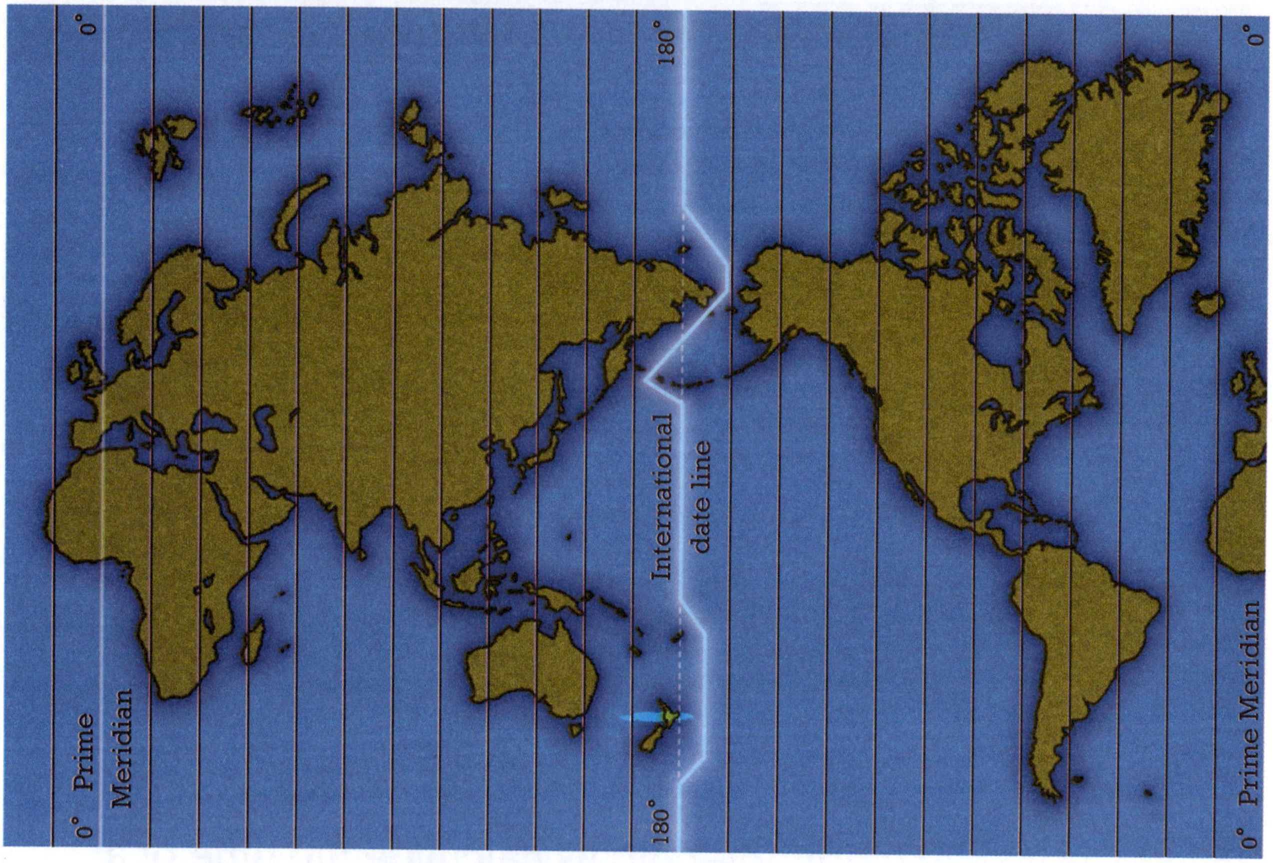

The International Date Line

The 180° longitude is also known as the **International Date Line**.

As we cross the International Date Line (IDL) from the east to the west, a day is subtracted. For example, if it is Sunday in New Delhi, it will be Saturday in New York. But if we cross the IDL from the west to the east, a day gets added. This line is not a straight one and has been drawn in an irregular manner in order to avoid cutting through inhabited land areas.

ISBN 978-81-8477-939-4

Explore

Consult the Internet or an atlas to find the time difference between the following places.

a. New York and Los Angeles
b. New Delhi and Beijing
c. London and Kolkata

Circle Time

Find out what is meant by the term 'jet lag'. Has any student in class ever experienced it? Have a class discussion on what causes jet lag.

Quiz Time

1. Fill in the blanks to complete the following sentences.

a. The __________ divides the Earth into two halves—the Northern and Southern hemispheres.

b. The __________ divides the Earth into the Western and Eastern hemispheres.

c. __________ are the imaginary lines that run across the Earth from west to east.

d. As the latitudes and the longitudes criss-cross the Earth, they form squares or a __________.

e. __________ help us calculate the local time of a place.

 ISBN 978-81-8477-939-4

2. On a world map, mark the following latitudes and longitudes.

a. The Tropic of Cancer

b. The Tropic of Capricorn

c. The Antarctic Circle

d. The Equator

e. The Greenwich Meridian

3. Draw lines to match items in Column A with those in Column B.

	A			B
a.	Tropic of Capricorn	•	•	180° longitude
b.	Prime Meridian	•	•	Northern Hemisphere
c.	Equator	•	•	Greenwich
d.	Tropic of Cancer	•	•	0° latitude
e.	International Date Line	•	•	Southern Hemisphere

4. Answer the questions.

a. What is a latitude? Name the important latitudes.

b. What is a longitude? Name the important longitudes.

c. What is the significance of the International Date Line? Support your answer with an example.

d. How does the 0° longitude divide the Earth?

What are the main differences between latitudes and longitudes?

 ISBN 978-81-8477-939-4

3 MOVEMENTS OF THE EARTH

There are two important movements that affect the Earth—rotation and revolution. The spinning of the Earth on its axis is called **rotation**. The Earth's rotation causes day and night. The movement of the Earth in its orbit around the Sun is called **revolution**. The Earth's revolution causes seasons during the year.

ROTATION

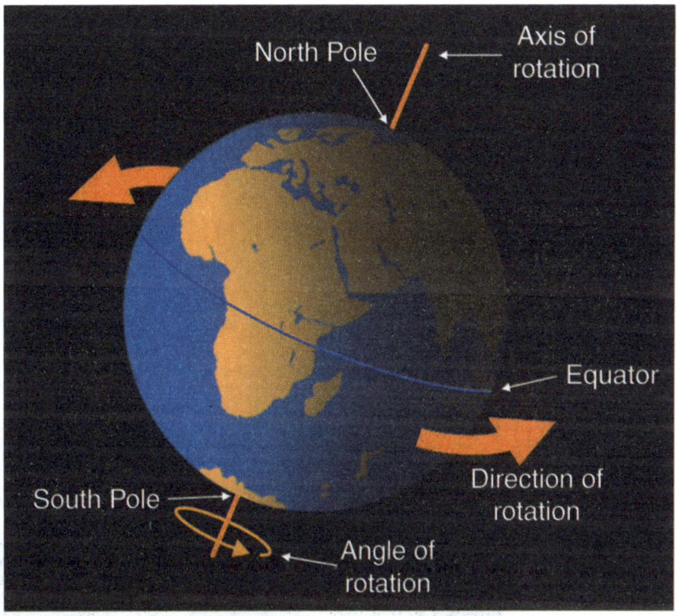

The Earth rotates around an invisible axis. The axis is tilted at 23.5°. It takes the Earth about twenty-four hours to complete one rotation. As it rotates, some parts of the Earth face the Sun and get light. These parts have day. The parts of the Earth not facing the Sun have night. The change from day to night and back again goes on continuously. Each rotation causes one complete day and night.

Factastic
The Earth rotates around its axis at the rate of about 1670 km per hour as it completes one rotation in twenty-four hours.

The Earth spins from west to east. As a result, the Sun

 ISBN 978-81-8477-939-4

appears to rise in the east and set in the west.

The rotation of the Earth influences the ocean currents and direction of winds. It also causes tides, that is, the rhythmic rise and fall of the ocean water twice a day.

> **Factastic**
> From the North Pole it appears that the Earth moves counter-clockwise. However, from the South Pole it seems that the Earth spins clockwise.

Revolution

The Earth's revolution around the Sun is in an elliptical orbit. One revolution takes 365 ¼ days, or one year.

> **Factastic**
> It takes the Earth approximately 365 days to go around the Sun once. This means that the Earth is speeding in space at a rate of about 107,279 km per hour!

Explore

Find information about leap years.

The Earth is closest to the Sun in early January each year. This is known as the 'perihelion'. The Earth is furthest from the Sun in early July each year. This is known as the 'aphelion'. The exact dates for perihelion and aphelion vary each year.

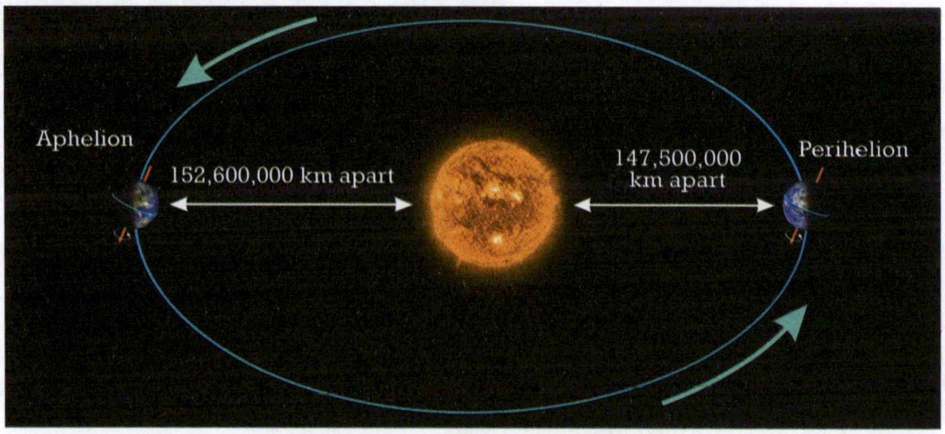

Apehelion and perihelion

 ISBN 978-81-8477-939-4

Just like the Earth, the other planets in our solar system also orbit the Sun. The time taken and the distance covered by these planets as they revolve around the Sun depend on their distance from the Sun.

Explore

Find out about the time taken by the other planets of the solar system to complete one rotation and one revolution. You can use the Internet or an encyclopedia to find this information. Discuss your observations in class.

LENGTH OF A DAY

The length of a day is calculated by the length of time the Sun is above the horizon. The length of the day changes through the year as the position of the Earth changes with respect to the Sun.

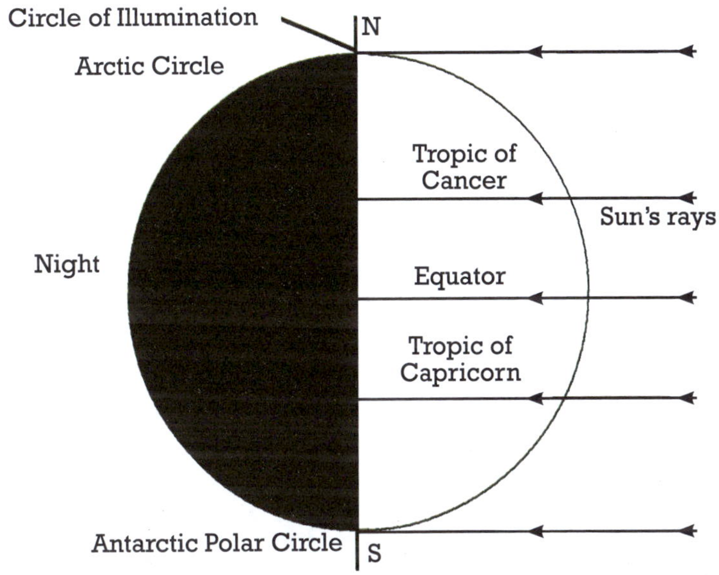

The imaginary circle that separates day from night on the globe is called the **Circle of Illumination**.

Circle Time

What would happen if one day the Sun did not rise? What would happen to us? What would be the temperature on Earth?

 ISBN 978-81-8477-939-4

Solstices

Twice in a year, the tilt of the Earth's axis reaches its maximum angle in relation to the Sun. This usually happens around 21 June and 22 December. These days are known as **solstices.** On the solstices, the Sun shines directly on one of the two tropics.

Around 21 June, the Northern Hemisphere leans towards the Sun. This date is known as the summer solstice and is the longest day of the year for places located north of the Tropic of Cancer. The North Pole leans towards the Sun, creating a twenty-four hour period of daylight (also known as the **polar day**). The South Pole, as it leans away from the Sun, experiences a twenty-four hour night, known as the **polar night**.

The winter solstice occurs on 22 December when the North Pole is leaning away from the Sun, and the South Pole is leaning towards the Sun. Places in the Northern Hemisphere experience the shortest day. Places in the Southern Hemisphere experience the longest day.

During the June solstice (summer solstice), the Sun shines directly on the Tropic of Cancer. During the December solstice (winter solstice), the Sun's rays shine on the Tropic of Capricorn.

Learn More

Explain with the help of diagrams why the North Pole and South Pole experience six months of day and six months of night.

 ISBN 978-81-8477-939-4

Equinoxes

As the Earth revolves around in its orbit, it reaches two points during a year when the tilt of its axis causes it to be straight relative to the Sun. These days are known as **equinoxes**. During the equinoxes, the rays of the Sun shine directly on the Equator. Day and night are of equal length everywhere on Earth. This happens around 21 March (spring or vernal equinox) and 23 September (autumn equinox).

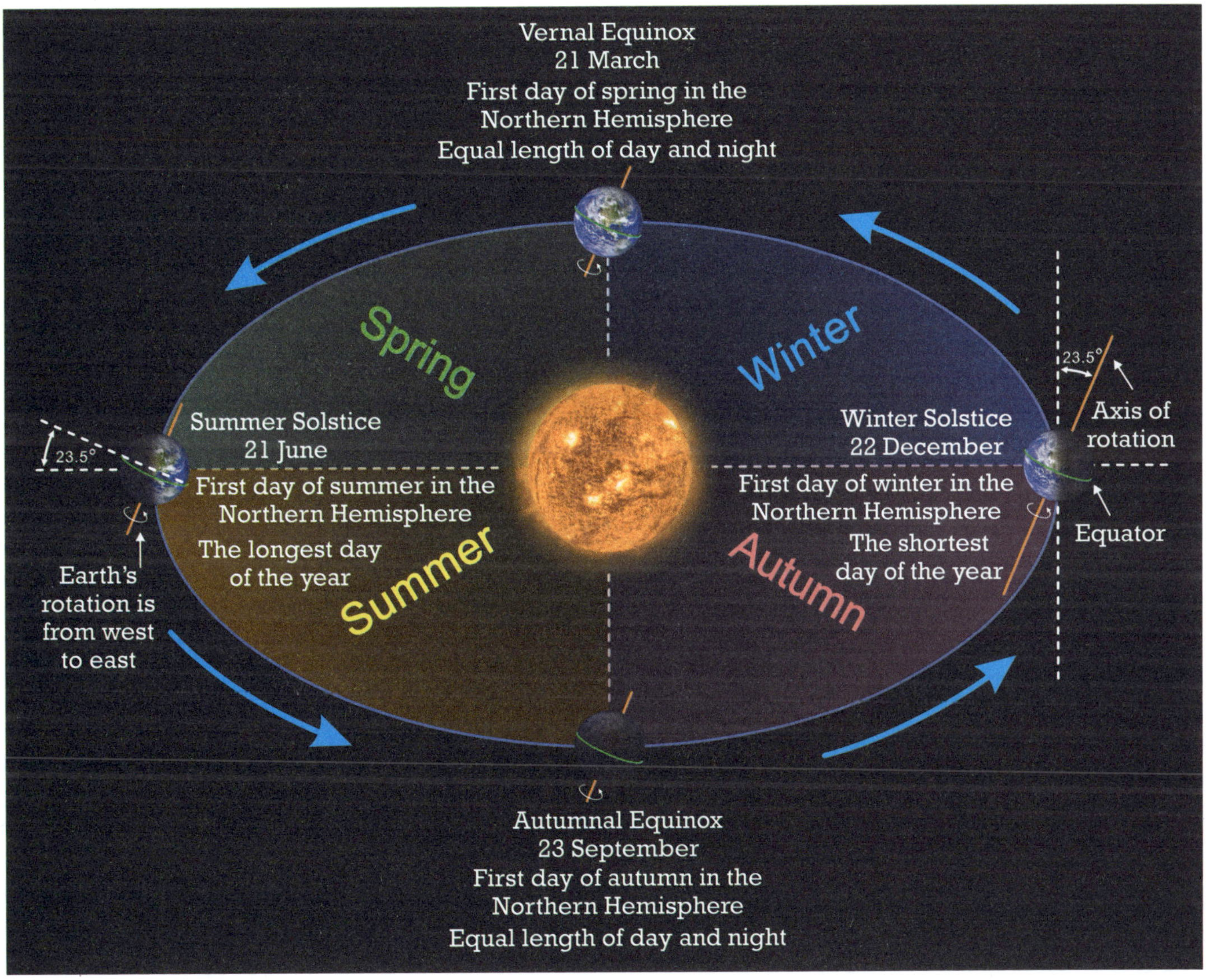

Solstices and Equinoxes

 ISBN 978-81-8477-939-4

Earth–Sun Relations and Seasons

	March Equinox	June Solstice	September Equinox	December Solstice
Date	21 March	21 June	23 September	22 December
Direct rays of the Sun fall on	Equator	Tropic of Cancer	Equator	Tropic of Capricorn
Length of day	12-hour day everywhere	24 hours of daylight at the North Pole; 24 hours of darkness at the South Pole; 12 hours of daylight at the Equator	12-hour day everywhere	24 hours of darkness at the North Pole; 24 hours of daylight at the South Pole; 12 hours of daylight at the Equator

Circle Time

Many cultures celebrate solstices and equinoxes. Find out about these celebrations with the aid of an encyclopedia or the Internet. Have a class discussion.

 ISBN 978-81-8477-939-4

SEASONS

The combined effect of the Earth's revolution and rotation results in the seasons. There are four main seasons on Earth—spring, summer, autumn and winter. As the Earth revolves around the Sun, one part of the Earth is tilted away from the Sun, while the other part leans towards the Sun. The part that is tilted away from the Sun experiences winter while the part that is leaning towards the Sun experiences summer. The seasons in between summer and winter are autumn and spring.

Quiz Time

1. Indicate whether the following statements are true (T) or false (F).

a. The Circle of Illumination is an imaginary circle that separates day from night. ☐

b. In the Northern Hemisphere, the vernal equinox takes place on 21 March. ☐

c. During the December solstice, the Sun's rays shine on the Tropic of Cancer. ☐

d. The rotation of the Earth influences the ocean currents. ☐

e. The fixed path on which the Earth revolves is known as the axis. ☐

f. The word equinox means unequal day and night. ☐

 ISBN 978-81-8477-939-4

2. **Define the following.**

a. Axis

b. Seasons

c. Circle of Illumination

d. Revolution of the Earth

3. **Answer the questions.**

a. What is the importance of the Sun to life on Earth?

b. Explain the two movements of the Earth. Support your answer with illustrations. How do the movements of the Earth affect us?

c. What are the summer and winter solstices?

d. What are the spring and autumn equinoxes?

Does the tilt of the Earth's axis play an important role in the seasons experienced on Earth? Give reasons for your answer.

 ISBN 978-81-8477-939-4

4

THE TEMPERATURE ZONES

The **weather** of a place includes the changes in temperature, air pressure, rain and wind conditions. It could change within a very short span of time or daily. The **climate** of a place or a region is the weather of that place or region over a long period of time.

The climate of any region is greatly influenced by the following:

- latitude
- altitude
- proximity to a large water body
- prevailing winds

LATITUDE OR THE DISTANCE FROM THE EQUATOR

Different latitudes receive different amounts of heat. The further away a place is from the Equator, the less heat it receives. Near the Equator, the rays of the Sun fall vertically, but near the poles, they are slanting.

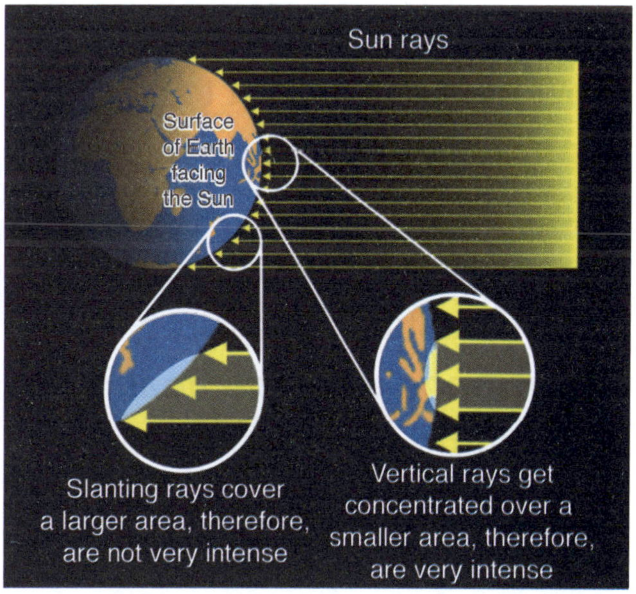

The vertical rays of the Sun focus on a smaller area and,

ISBN 978-81-8477-939-4

therefore, provide a lot of heat. The slanting rays of the Sun, on the other hand, are spread over a greater area and do not provide as much heat.

Therefore, places located close to the Equator are very hot while those located close to the poles are cooler.

Altitude

The air around us is not heated directly by the Sun's rays; instead, the Sun's rays heat the Earth, and the Earth heats the air. As we go to higher altitudes, the amount of heat received from the Earth's surface decreases and so it is cooler up there.

Proximity to a Water Body

Coastal areas have a lower temperature range than areas that are inland. This is because land heats and cools faster than the sea. As the land heats up in the summer, cool sea breezes blow in from the sea to cool the land. In the winter season, the warm sea breezes blow towards the land. Coastal areas rarely experience extreme heat or cold, while inland areas do.

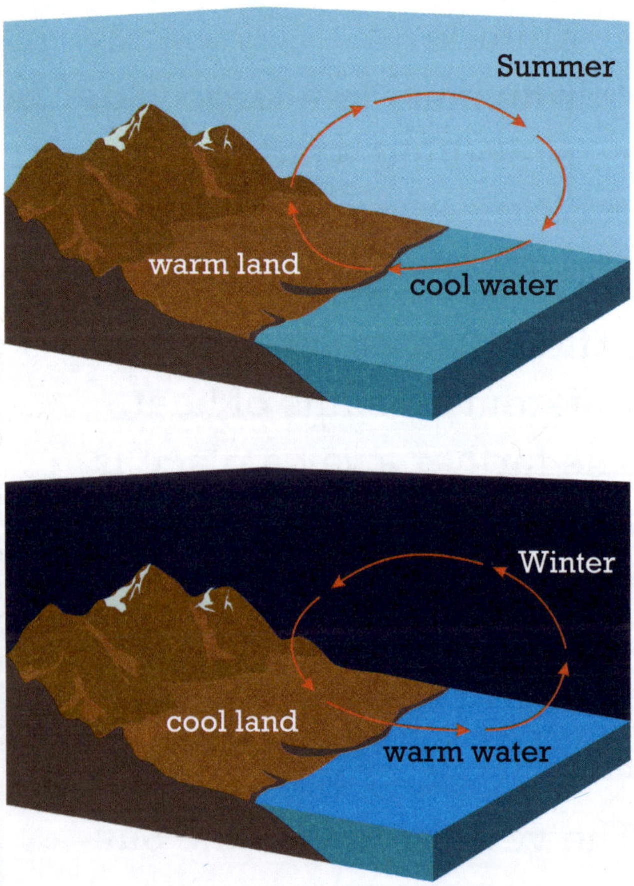

Sea and land breezes

 ISBN 978-81-8477-939-4

WINDS

Winds greatly affect the climate of a particular place depending on their place of origin. Winds blowing from the sea are cool while those blowing from the deserts are hot.

Explore

Find out what the climate of the Earth was like when it was born.

EARTH'S TEMPERATURE ZONES

The Earth is divided into temperature zones according to the amount of heat they receive:

- The Torrid Zone
- The Temperate Zone
- The Frigid Zone

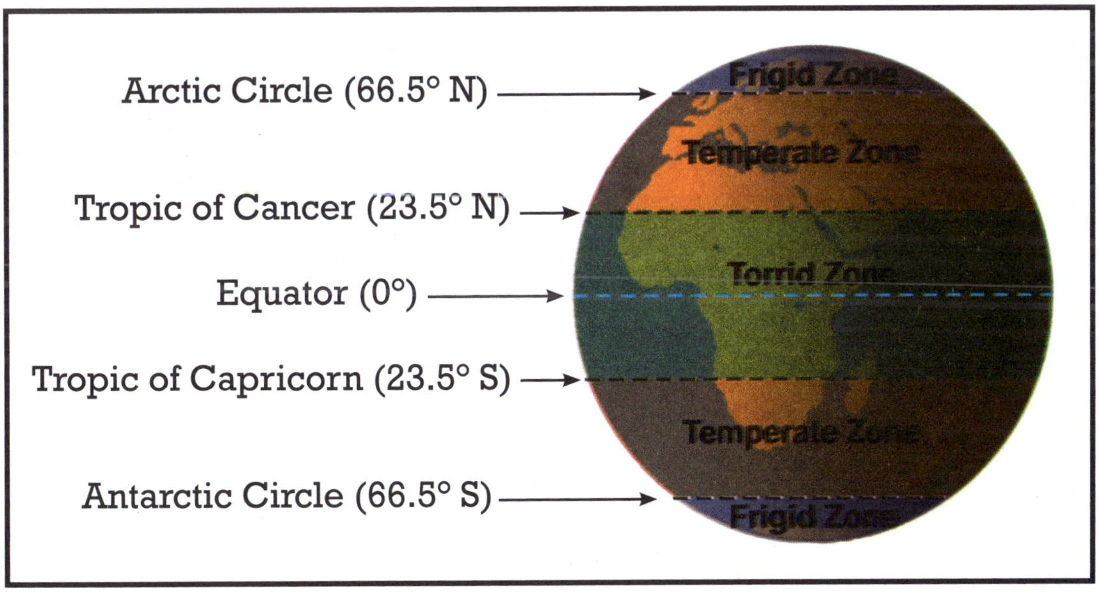

 ISBN 978-81-8477-939-4

The Torrid Zone

The tropical or the Torrid Zone

The region between the Tropic of Cancer (23.5° N) and the Tropic of Capricorn (23.5° S) is known as the Torrid Zone or the hot zone. The Torrid Zone extends over both the Northern and the Southern hemispheres. It is also called the tropical zone.

The Sun's rays fall vertically over this region almost throughout the year. As a result, it experiences a hot climate without much variation throughout the year.

The Temperate Zone

A temperate forest

The regions between the Tropic of Cancer (23.5° N) and the Arctic Circle (66.5° N) in the Northern Hemisphere and the Tropic of Capricorn (23.5° S) and Antarctic Circle (66.5° S) in the Southern Hemisphere form the Temperate Zone. This zone experiences mild temperatures as the Sun's rays fall on the Earth's surface at an angle throughout the year. The days are longer during the summer months, while the nights are longer in the winter months.

 ISBN 978-81-8477-939-4

THE FRIGID ZONE

Frigid Zone

The region between the Arctic Circle (66.5° N) and the North Pole (90° N) in the Northern Hemisphere, and between the Antarctic Circle (66.5° S) and the South Pole (90° S) in the Southern Hemisphere is known as the Frigid Zone. The Sun's rays fall at a sharp angle throughout the year. This makes the Frigid Zone extremely cold all year round.

Circle Time

Have a class discussion on the kinds of clothes people wear in the different temperature zones of Earth.

Learn More

On a physical map of the world, mark the Torrid Zone, the Temperate Zone and the Frigid Zone.

Explore

Look up an encyclopedia and list one animal and one plant found exclusively in each of the temperature zones of Earth.

 ISBN 978-81-8477-939-4

Quiz Time

1. **Fill in the blanks to complete the following sentences.**

a. The distribution of temperature is not ____________ on the surface of the Earth.

b. The Sun's rays fall at an inclined ______________ in the Frigid Zone.

c. The longest latitude in between the Tropic of Cancer and the Tropic of Capricorn is the ____________.

2. **Indicate whether the following statements are true (T) or false (F).**

a. Places near the Equator receive less heat from the Sun. ☐

b. The Torrid Zone experiences all the four seasons. ☐

c. The higher the altitude of a place, the hotter it gets. ☐

d. Summer days are short in the Temperate Zone. ☐

e. Sea breezes have a cooling effect on coastal areas. ☐

3. **List four factors that influence the climate of a region.**

4. **Write fifty words on each of the following.**

a. The Temperate Zone

b. The Frigid Zone

c. The Torrid Zone

Ooty, in south India, is located close to the Equator. Yet, it experiences a cool climate throughout the year. Why?

 ISBN 978-81-8477-939-4

5
The Equatorial Forests

The equatorial forest region forms a part of the Torrid Zone. It lies across the Equator between 0° to 23.5° North and South of the Equator. It is spread over parts of Asia, Africa and South America.

In South America, the region includes the Amazon lowlands and coastal lowlands of northeastern Brazil, coastal Colombia and parts of Ecuador. In Africa, it covers the entire Zaire (Congo) Basin and the Guinea Coast in West Africa. In Asia, it covers Malaysia, Singapore, Indonesia, Papua New Guinea, parts of Philippines, peninsular Thailand and parts of Sri Lanka and India.

World's equatorial forests

 ISBN 978-81-8477-939-4

Explore

List the countries that fall in the equatorial forest region.

Climate

The Sun's rays fall directly over the equatorial forest region throughout the year. As a result, the region has a hot and humid climate. This is known as equatorial climate.

The days and nights are of equal duration. The temperature during the day is around 30°C to 35°C. At night, it drops between 20°C to 25°C. There is very little difference between the warmest and coolest months. The temperature stays warm throughout the year.

This region receives heavy rainfall all year round. The rainfall is especially heavy around the equinoxes in March and September. Places that are further from the Equator get less rainfall. The region also gets several thunderstorms.

Plant Life

The warm temperature and heavy rainfall make the region hot, humid and damp. Such conditions produce lush vegetation in this region. The growing, fruit-bearing and shedding period of the different trees found in these forests differ. As a result, all the trees do not shed their leaves at the same time. These forests, therefore, always appear lush and green and are referred to as evergreen forests.

 ISBN 978-81-8477-939-4

Many different varieties of trees grow in the equatorial forests. The trees found here include mahogany, rosewood, ebony, cinchona and rubber. Palms and tree ferns are also found in the region. Mangrove forests cover large parts of coastal areas and swamps.

The evergreen equatorial forests cover nearly 7 million square km of the Earth's surface. They absorb a lot of carbon dioxide from the atmosphere and release a large amount of oxygen. They are, therefore, known as the 'Lungs of the Earth'.

Layers of the Forest

The rainforests are made up of four layers.

The emergent layer: This is the topmost layer. This section comprises very tall trees. The tallest trees are as tall as 60 m above the forest floor. Their trunks can be as thick as 5 m. Most of the trees in the emergent layer have broad leaves that help them absorb sunlight. Animals such as eagles, monkeys, bats and butterflies are found in this layer.

The canopy: The canopy is the second layer. It forms a kind of roof of the forest. It grows beneath the emergent layer. It rises to 45 m above the forest floor. The trees in this layer have smooth, oval leaves. The leaves let rainwater slip quickly. Many animals live in this layer. They include snakes, toucans and tree frogs.

The understory: The understory is the third layer. Plants in this layer grow to about 3.5 m. They receive very little sunlight because of the dense canopy above them. Ferns, creepers,

 ISBN 978-81-8477-939-4

orchids and grass grow in this layer. Animals in this layer include jaguars, red-eyed tree frogs and leopards. A large variety of insects are also found in this layer.

The rainforest floor: This is the lowest layer of the forest. Almost no sunlight reaches this layer making it very dark. Hardly any plants are able to grow here. It is covered with leaves that rot quickly. The rotting leaves are food for insects such as termites, cockroaches, beetles, scorpions and earthworms. Giant anteaters are also found in this layer.

An equatorial forest

Circle Time

The equatorial rainforests provide up to 40 per cent of the oxygen found in the atmosphere. Discuss ways in which the rainforests can be preserved.

 ISBN 978-81-8477-939-4

Learn More

Make your own earthworm pit. Find and collect a few earthworms from the school garden. Place the earthworms in a transparent glass jar full of soil. Place degradable food stuff such as banana peels, apple cores or spinach leaves in the jar. Note your observations for four weeks.

WILDLIFE

Jaguar

About half of all animal species found on Earth live in the tropical rainforests. There are a large number of insects such as butterflies, termites, mosquitoes, spiders, ticks, gnats and tsetse flies in the equatorial forests. The region is home to many animals that live on trees, such as monkeys, gorillas, sloths, bats, tree frogs, tree lizards, green iguanas and flying squirrels. Animals such as jaguars and some species of snakes find their prey among the tree-dwelling animals.

Gorilla

Anaconda

The rivers and swamps of the equatorial region are home to alligators, crocodiles and

 ISBN 978-81-8477-939-4

hippopotamuses. Large animals, such as rhinoceroses and elephants, are able to make their way through the thick rainforest undergrowth. The rainforests also have many species of birds, such as toucans, parrots, macaws and hummingbirds.

Toucan

Macaw

Factastic

The Amazonian rainforest in South America is the oldest tropical forest in the world. It is around 55 million years old. Almost one-sixth of the world's broad-leaf forests are found in the Amazon.

Learn More

Imagine you are planning a holiday in the equatorial forest. Make a list of the things that you will need to pack. Provide reasons for including those items.

Human Life

Equatorial regions are sparsely populated because of the extremely hot conditions. Insect and waterborne diseases are quite common in these forests.

A few tribal communities are found in these forests. Most of them are nomadic. They hunt, gather fruits and nuts, and fish in order to survive. They include the Pygmies of the Congo Basin, the Kubus of Sumatra and the Semangs of Malaysia.

Other native tribal communities, such as the Dayaks of Borneo, the Bantus of Zaire and the Indians of the Amazonian region, practise shifting agriculture.

 ISBN 978-81-8477-939-4

Learn More

Find out about the tribes native to the equatorial forests. Make a presentation in class on any one tribe. Discuss where they live, their diet, their main occupations, the kinds of houses they live in and their culture. Your presentation can be in the form of a chart, a file or a computer display.

Farming and Agriculture

The soil in the rainforests is not very fertile. The frequent rain causes floods. As a result, the conditions are not favourable for farming.

The native people of the region clear an area of the forest and cultivate it with food crops. They grow only as much as they need for their families. When the soil loses its fertility, they move to a new area. This is called **subsistence** or **shifting** agriculture.

In some places, now, crops are grown for sale in the market. They are grown on a large farm or estate. This is called **plantation agriculture**. Plantation crops include rubber, cotton, oil, coffee, sugar cane and oilseeds. These crops are not cultivated for immediate consumption. Rather, they are grown to be sold for money.

 ISBN 978-81-8477-939-4

Explore

Use an atlas and find the names of five cities located in the equatorial region. Make a project on any one of these cities. Mention the location of the city, its climate, its economy and the reasons why it is important.

Quiz Time

1. Draw lines to match the terms given in Column A with their descriptions given in Column B.

A	B
a. Emergent layer •	• Ferns, creepers, orchids and grass grow in this layer
b. Canopy •	• Almost no sunlight reaches this layer
c. Understory •	• This layer forms a kind of roof of the forest
d. Rainforest floor •	• This is the topmost layer of the forest

2. Indicate whether the following statements are true (T) or false (F).

a. The equatorial regions are sparsely populated because of the extremely hot conditions. ☐

b. The soil in the rainforests is very fertile. ☐

 ISBN 978-81-8477-939-4

c. The Sun's rays fall direct over the equatorial forest region throughout the year. ☐

d. The rainforests have many species of birds, such as toucans, parrots, macaws and hummingbirds. ☐

e. Snow leopards, bears and kangaroos are found in large numbers in the equatorial forests. ☐

3. Fill in the blanks to complete the following sentences.

a. The equatorial forest region lies between ________ ° N and ________ ° S.

b. The equatorial rainforests are known as the '________ of the Earth'.

c. Animals such as eagles, monkeys, bats and butterflies are found in the ________ layer of equatorial forests.

d. The Torrid Zone receives very heavy rainfall especially around the ________.

4. Answer the questions.

a. What kind of climate prevails in the equatorial forests?

b. Write a short note on the kind of agriculture practised in the equatorial region.

c. Why is the human population in the equatorial forests sparse?

d. Provide a brief description of the layers of the equatorial forest.

Why is it vital that we preserve the equatorial forests?

 ISBN 978-81-8477-939-4

6
THE DESERTS

Deserts cover more than one-fifth of the Earth's surface. They are found in every continent. Deserts are areas of land that are dry and barren. Desert areas receive very little rainfall.

More than one billion people, that is, one-sixth of the Earth's population, actually live in desert regions.

There are two types of deserts on the Earth—hot deserts and cold deserts.

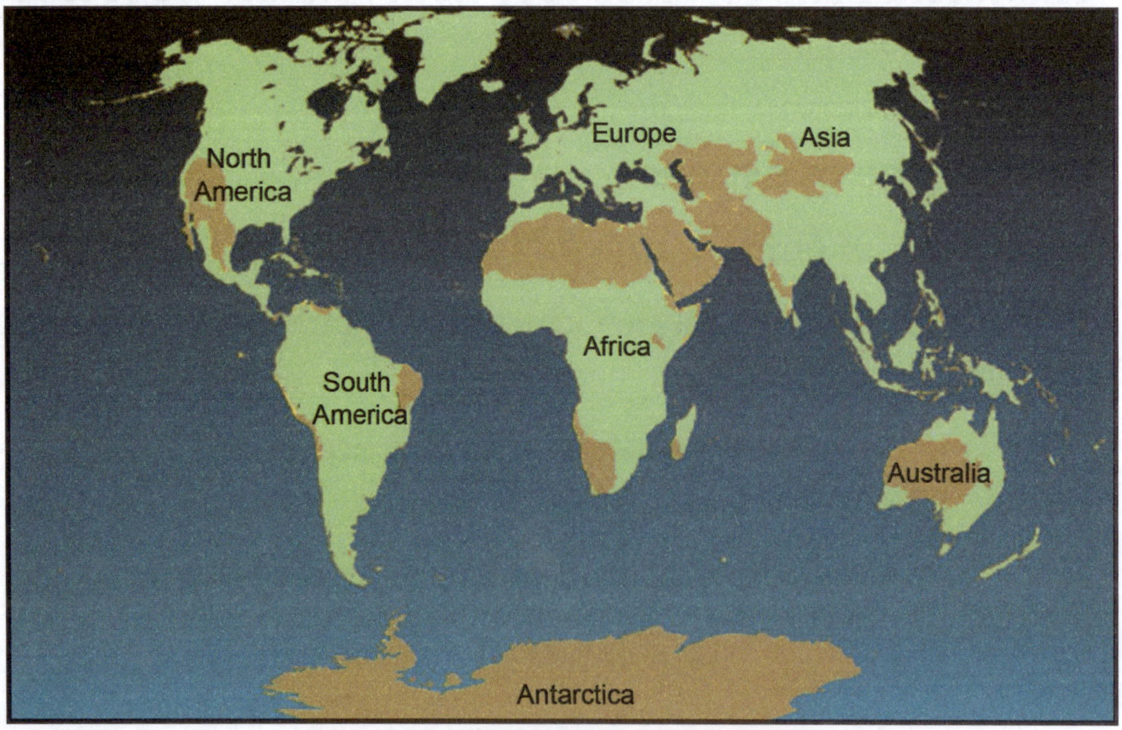

World's deserts (hot and cold)

 ISBN 978-81-8477-939-4

Hot Deserts

Most of the Earth's hot deserts are located around the Tropic of Cancer and the Tropic of Capricorn. The deserts are mostly located on the western side of the continents in which they are found.

The Earth's hot deserts include the Sahara and the Kalahari deserts in Africa, the Atacama Desert in South America, the Mexican Desert in Mexico, the Thar Desert in India and the Australian Desert in Australia.

Climate

Hot deserts have a warm climate throughout the year. They get very hot in summer. The winter sometimes brings little rainfall but this rainwater evaporates almost immediately. Often, rainwater evaporates even before it reaches the ground. Precipitation is usually less than 250 mm in a year.

The temperatures are extreme. The maximum temperature goes over 45°C. The minimum temperature can drop as low as –18°C.

Factastic

The highest temperature ever recorded was 56.7°C in Death Valley, California, USA.

It rarely rains in the deserts. When it does, it is accompanied by thunderstorms. Desert skies are usually cloudless. This causes daytime temperatures to rise rapidly. At night, temperatures drop significantly.

 ISBN 978-81-8477-939-4

Soil

Soil in hot deserts is coarse, rocky or gravelly. Fine dust and sand particles get blown around in sandstorms.

Thar Desert

Sahara Desert

Sanora Desert, Mexico

Australian Desert

Atacama Desert

Kalahari Desert

 ISBN 978-81-8477-939-4

Circle Time

The temperatures in the deserts can range from 20°C at four o'clock in the afternoon to 0°C at four o'clock in the morning. Discuss why this is so.

Factastic

'Drought evaders' are desert plants that exist as seeds before the rain. They grow as soon as the rain arrives, produce flowers and seeds and then die. Hence, they live only when there is a lot of water. Drought evaders include cottonwood trees, willows, ferns and poison ivy. 'Drought resistors' are plants that have adapted to survive long periods without water, for example, the baobab tree.

Plant Life

Very few plants are able to withstand the extreme temperatures and lack of water in hot deserts. The few plants that are found here have adaptations that help them survive in the extreme conditions of hot deserts. Some plants have long roots that reach deep within the soil to absorb underground water. The leaves of some plants are small, thick and covered with a waxy outer layer. This helps the plants retain water. Some plants store water in their fleshy stems or leaves. Such plants are called succulents. The leaves of cacti are reduced to spines. These help the plants reduce water loss due to transpiration. They also protect the plants from grazing animals. Desert plants include yuccas, cacti, turpentine bush, fairy dusters, prickly pears, agaves, mormon tea and brittlebush.

Fairy duster

Mormon tea

Pipe cactus

 ISBN 978-81-8477-939-4

Animal Life

Ostrich

A large variety of animals, birds and insects, such as camels, foxes, hyenas, rats, snakes, burros, roadrunners and ostriches are found in the hot deserts.

Wild burro

Desert animals have adapted ways to help them keep cool and use less water. Camels, for example, can go for days without food and water. Many desert animals are nocturnal, coming out to hunt only when the Sun has set. Some animals, like the desert tortoise spend much of their time underground. Most desert birds are nomadic, criss-crossing the skies in search of food.

Kangaroo rat

Roadrunner

Grey fox

Mountain lion

Explore

Find ten fascinating facts about deserts from an encyclopedia or the Internet.

 ISBN 978-81-8477-939-4

Adaptation of the Camel to Life in the Hot Deserts

The camel is well-adapted to surviving in an extremely hot and dry desert. It can survive without drinking water for nearly three months. After a period without water, a thirsty camel is able to drink several litres of water at a time. The camel's body is adapted to retaining water. It does not sweat much.

Camels

The hump on the camel's back is an adaptation for coping with scarce food in the desert. The hump stores fat that the camel uses to survive when there is no food to eat. The camel can survive without eating for several weeks.

Factastic

The camel walks in a different way from other animals. It moves the two right-side legs together followed by the two left-side legs. This causes the noticeable 'swinging' of its rider.

The camel has large, broad feet that do not sink in the sand. It has double rows of long eyelashes that keep sand out of its eyes. Its eyes have a thin clear membrane that acts like a transparent eyelid. It protects the camel's eyes from sandstorms while still letting in enough light for the camel to see. The camel's ears are small and rounded. They are located at the back of its head and are covered with hair. The hair shelters its ears from sand.

 ISBN 978-81-8477-939-4

Human Life

A Bedouin man

Human population in the deserts is very sparse. The extreme temperatures of the deserts make it difficult for people to live there. The Bedouins of north Africa and Saudi Arabia and the Tuaregs of Western Sahara live in the hot deserts.

The main occupations of people who live in desert regions are animal rearing, farming and mining. People in the deserts live a nomadic life, that is, they move from one place to another in search of food, water and other resources. Human settlements in deserts are primarily near oases or other water bodies like rivers. Summer crops grown in these regions are rice, maize and millet. Lentils, barley, beans and wheat are crops grown in winter.

Cold Deserts

Besides hot deserts, there are temperate deserts, such as the Gobi Desert of Mongolia. Cold deserts are found between the Poles and the Arctic and Antarctic circles, such as the tundra in Russia. The cool deserts of central Asia have a very extreme climate, with hot summers and very cold winters. The cold deserts, also known as the polar deserts, experience a cold climate throughout the year.

Learn More

On a physical map of the world, mark out the hot deserts in yellow and the cold deserts in pink. Label the deserts.

oases: small, fertile or green areas in a desert region, where water is found

 ISBN 978-81-8477-939-4

Climate

Cold deserts have extremely cold winters and short, cool summers. The main form of precipitation is snow rather than rain. Precipitation is less than 50 cm in a year.

Antarctica is the Earth's largest cold desert. It is covered with a thick, permanent ice sheet. The temperature in Antarctica can get as low as –89°C. In the Arctic, the temperatures can be as low as –67.8°C.

Plant Life

The permanently frozen land does not allow the growth of plants and trees. The main vegetation is moss, lichen and short grasses. In the tundra region, some flowering plants grow in the short summer.

Animal Life

Animals found in cold deserts include polar bear, reindeer (also called caribou in North America), Arctic fox and penguins. They have adapted to surviving in extremely cold conditions.

Penguins in Antarctica

Reindeer

 ISBN 978-81-8477-939-4

Adaptations of the Polar Bear to the Cold Deserts

Polar bear

The polar bear has many adaptations that help it cope with the freezing cold desert climate. It has a thick double layer of fur that helps it keep warm.

Under its furry coat, the polar bear has black skin. As dark colours absorb more heat than light colours, the black skin helps trap heat within the polar bear's body. Under its skin, the polar bear has a thick layer of fat called blubber that insulates its body. The fur on its feet keeps the polar bear warm and keeps it from slipping on the slippery ice. Five sharp, curved claws on each foot help the polar bear grasp the ice.

The polar bear's white fur acts as a camouflage in the Arctic environment. It is able to blend with the white snow all around and stay hidden when it stalks its prey. When prey is hard to find, the polar bear uses up the reserves of fat in its body.

People in Cold Deserts

A Mongolian settlement

Very few people live in cold deserts. There are no permanent residents in Antarctica. Small populations live near the tundra. They include the Inuit in Alaska, the Lapps in Lapland and the Yakuts in North Asia.

The native people have adapted to life in the cold deserts. They build temporary houses or live in tents. They hunt animals for food.

 ISBN 978-81-8477-939-4

Learn More

Make a project on any group native to the hot or cold deserts. Find out about where they live, their habitation, diet and culture. Find out about their main occupation and their culture. Make a presentation in class.

Quiz Time

1. **Fill in the blanks to complete the sentences.**

a. The Earth's hot deserts are mostly found on the ________ side of the continents in which they are located.

b. Some desert plants have long ________ that reach deep within the soil to absorb underground water.

c. In the ________ region, some flowering plants grow in the short summer.

d. The polar bear has a thick double ________ of fur that helps it keep warm.

e. The camel can survive without eating for several ________.

2. **Indicate whether the following statements are true (T) or false (F).**

a. Antarctica is the Earth's largest cold desert. ☐

b. In some places in a desert, the underground water comes to the surface and forms small fertile areas. ☐

c. Hot deserts have a warm climate only in summer. ☐

 ISBN 978-81-8477-939-4

d. There are several permanent residents in Antarctica. ☐

e. Under its furry coat, the polar bear has black skin. ☐

3. Answer the questions.

a. How are hot deserts similar to cold deserts?

b. Why is the desert climate very dry?

c. How do animals survive in extremely hot or cold conditions?

d. Write a short note on how the camel has adapted to life in the hot deserts.

e. Write a short note on plant and animal life in the cold deserts.

4. Draw lines to match the deserts listed in Column A with their location listed in Column B.

	A			B
a.	Atacama	•	•	Russia
b.	Thar	•	•	Mongolia
c.	Kalahari	•	•	India
d.	Gobi	•	•	Africa
e.	Tundra	•	•	South America

Why do you think most people in the desert regions are usually nomadic?

 ISBN 978-81-8477-939-4

7
The Temperate Zone

In the Northern Hemisphere, the Temperate Zone is the area located between the Tropic of Cancer and the Arctic Circle. In the Southern Hemisphere, it is located between the Tropic of Capricorn and the Antarctic Circle.

The North Temperate Zone includes Europe, northern parts of Asia, North America and the northern part of Mexico. The South Temperate Zone includes southern Australia, New Zealand, southern South America and South Africa.

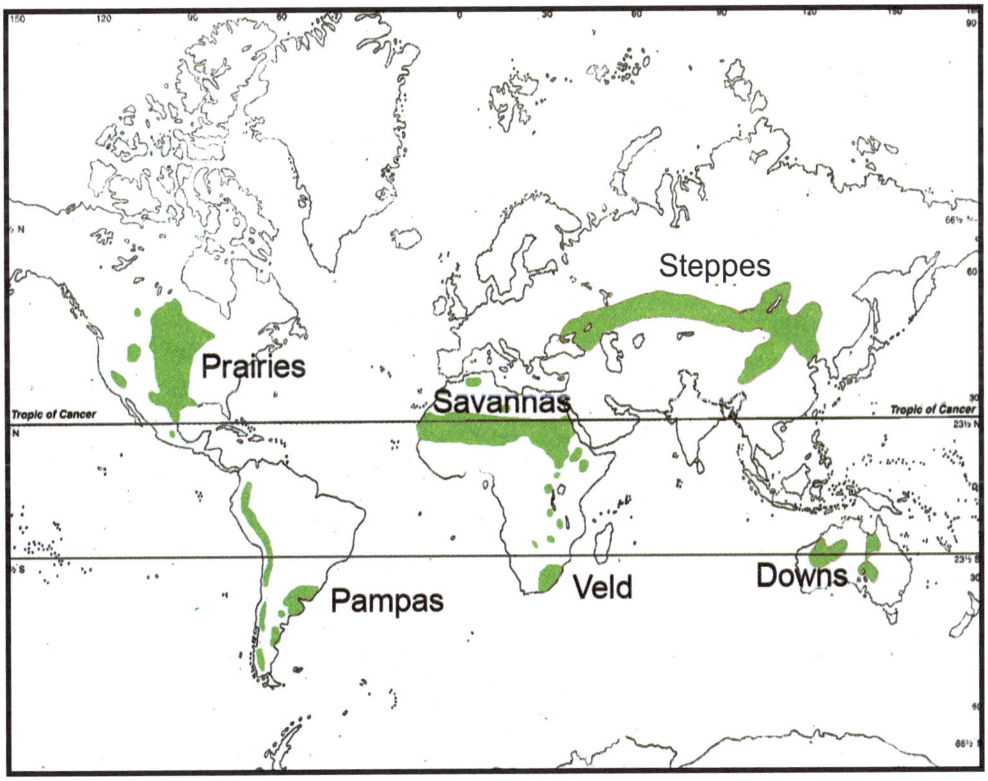

The grasslands of the Temperate Zone

 ISBN 978-81-8477-939-4

The temperate region is known for its grasslands that cover nearly one-third of the Earth's land surface. Grasslands are open, fairly flat and continuous areas made up of many different kinds of grasses. This area does not have enough regular rainfall to support the growth of a forest, but not so little as to form a desert.

These grasslands are known by different names in different countries.

The various grasslands are:

- Prairies in North America
- Steppes in Russia
- Pampas in South America
- Savannas in north Africa
- Velds in South Africa
- Downs in Australia

Explore

Find out how the grasslands of the Northern Hemisphere are different from those of the Southern Hemisphere.

CLIMATE

The Temperate Zone is divided into the Continental Temperate Zone and the Oceanic Temperate Zone. The Continental Temperate Zone has very cold winters. It receives very light rainfall in the winters. Eastern Europe is part of the Continental Temperate Zone.

 ISBN 978-81-8477-939-4

The Oceanic Temperate Zone is never extremely cold or hot. It receives a lot of rainfall. It also experiences severe storms and cyclones. The United States, China, parts of India, parts of Canada, Europe, and large parts of Russia lie in the Oceanic Temperate Zone in the Northern Hemisphere. New Zealand, parts of Australia, the southernmost tip of Africa and the southern tip of South America lie in the Oceanic Temperate Zone in the Southern Hemisphere.

Factastic
Grasslands exist in every continent except Antarctica.

Plant Life

Plant life in this region is essentially grass and some flowers. It varies from region to region, depending on the rainfall received. Since the Prairies in North America receive a lot of rain, the grass there is tall. The Steppes have shorter grass because they receive less rainfall. The colour of grass also varies during each season.

Explore

Look up the Internet or an encyclopedia and find out why the temperate grasslands are so fertile.

Wildlife

Jack rabbit

The animals that live in temperate grasslands have adapted to its dry, windy conditions. Animals found in this region include grazing animals, such as gazelles

 ISBN 978-81-8477-939-4

Antelope

Koala

Gazelle

and deer; burrowing animals, such as mice and jack rabbits; and predators such as snakes, coyotes and grizzly bears.

The African Savanna is home to elephants, giraffes, rhinos, zebras, lions, hyenas and warthogs.

In the grasslands of Australia, we can find koalas, wallabies and kangaroos.

Kangaroo

Elephants

Warthog

Zebra

 ISBN 978-81-8477-939-4

Human Impact

The Prairies in North America are known as the 'Granary of the World'. Crops, such as rye, wheat, oats and barley, are grown here. Agriculture is extensively mechanised here. Machines called combine harvesters are used to harvest the crop. Wheat is also grown in Canada, Russia and Australia.

Sheep shearing

Livestock ranching is also practised in the temperate grasslands. The open grasslands provide good natural pastures for the cattle. Livestock is raised in huge farms called ranches. Argentina is one of the leading exporters of meat and leather products.

Thresher

Circle Time

Bisons once freely roamed the Prairies in huge herds. Commercial hunting and slaughter reduced their numbers so dramatically that they nearly became extinct. Discuss with the class animal species that have been similarly threatened in India and the pros and cons of bringing forest land under agriculture.

 ISBN 978-81-8477-939-4

Dairy farming is another important occupation practised in the temperate grasslands. Farms produce fresh milk, butter, cheese and other milk products. Australia and New Zealand export dairy products to many countries around the world.

Learn More

Find out about tribes native to the temperate grasslands. Find out where they live, their diet and the nature of their habitation. Find out details about their culture and lifestyle. Present your findings in the form of an oral presentation, a booklet or a chart in class.

Quiz Time

1. Fill in the blanks to complete the sentences.

a. Kangaroos are found in ____________.

b. The Prairies are known as the '____________ of the World'.

c. Plant life in the grasslands comprises mainly ____________ and a few flowers.

d. Grasslands exist in every continent except ____________.

e. Grasslands cover ____________ of the Earth's land surface.

2. Answer the questions.

a. Where are most grasslands of the world located?

b. What are Velds?

 ISBN 978-81-8477-939-4

c. Why are the Prairies called the 'Granary of the World'?

d. Write a short note on the animal life found in temperate grasslands.

3. Draw lines to match the grasslands listed in Column A with their location in Column B

	A			B
a.	Russia	•	•	Velds
b.	Australia	•	•	Steppes
c.	South Africa	•	•	Downs
d.	South America	•	•	Prairies
e.	North America	•	•	Pampas

4. Indicate whether the following statements are true (T) or false (F).

a. Most of the grasslands of the world lie between the Equator and the Tropic of Cancer. ☐

b. The Prairies have hot summers and cold winters. ☐

c. The grasslands of South America are called the Downs. ☐

d. The natural vegetation of the temperate grasslands comprises tall trees and short shrubs. ☐

e. Dairy farming is an important occupation in the temperate grasslands. ☐

What are the factors that make agriculture and dairy farming the main occupations of the people living in the temperate grasslands?

 ISBN 978-81-8477-939-4

8
The Frigid Zone

The North Frigid Zone lies between the North Pole and the Arctic Circle. The South Frigid Zone lies between the South Pole and the Antarctic Circle. The Frigid Zone is also called the polar region or the Polar Zone.

The Frigid Zones are the coldest parts of the Earth. They are located far from the Equator. They do not receive a lot of sunlight. Vast areas are covered with ice and snow throughout the year.

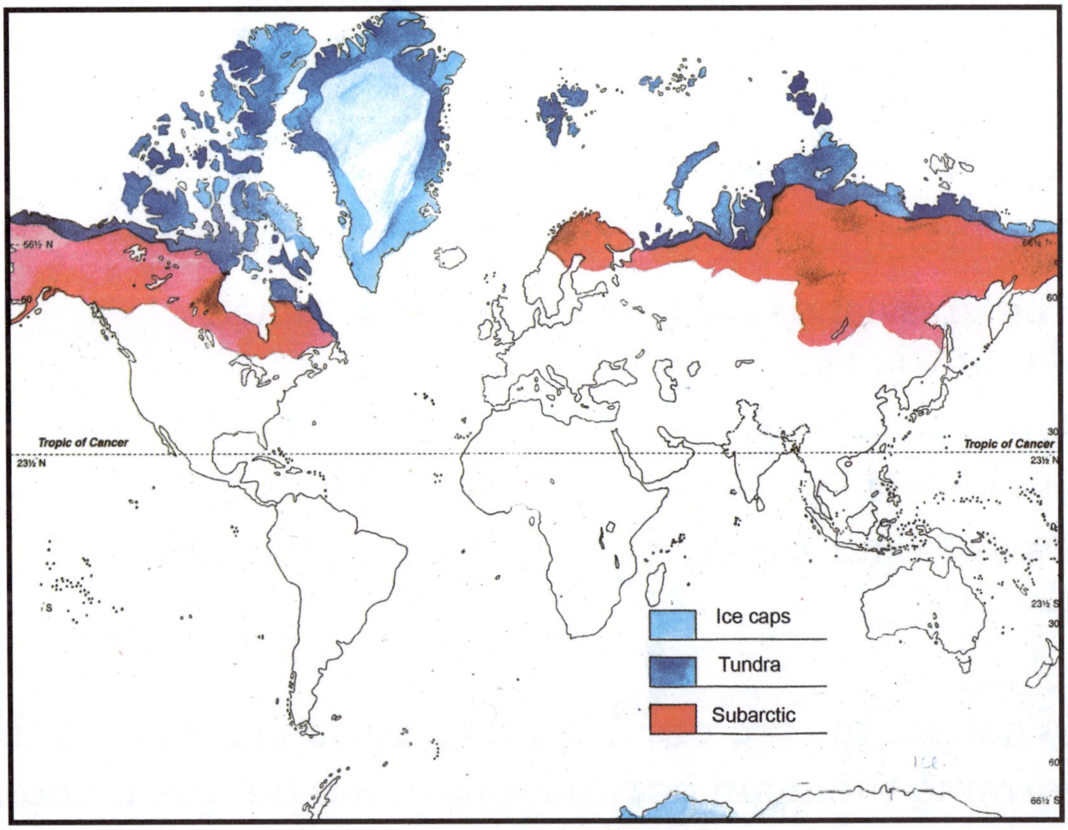

The Frigid Zone

 ISBN 978-81-8477-939-4

The zones experience long periods of daylight in summer and long periods of darkness in winter.

Factastic
Both the North Pole and the South Pole experience six months of continuous darkness during the winter and six months of light during the summer.

As the rays of the Sun fall at a very sharp angle in this region, it receives very little heat from the Sun.

Learn More

Find out which countries are referred to as the 'Land of the Midnight Sun' and why. Present your findings as an oral presentation, a chart or a computer display in class.

THE NORTH FRIGID ZONE OR THE ARCTIC REGION

The North Frigid Zone is the Arctic region. It includes northern Canada, Alaska, Greenland, northern Russia and large parts of Norway, Denmark, Sweden, Finland and Iceland. The Arctic Ocean lies in the North Frigid Zone.

A forest in Alaska

The North Pole lies at sea level in the the Arctic Ocean. The ocean water moderates the climate of this zone. The sea ice at the North Pole is about 2 m to 3 m thick.

 ISBN 978-81-8477-939-4

The zone has severely cold winters and cold summers. The average temperatures can be as low as –40°C in winter. The region is very dry. Precipitation is in the form of snow. The region experiences strong, dry winds that cause snowstorms.

Places located on coasts in the Arctic region are comparatively warmer. They receive heavier snowfall than the inland areas.

The South Frigid Zone or the Antarctic Region

The South Frigid Zone comprises the continent of Antarctica. It is covered by permanently frozen ground. This is called **permafrost**. The large continent reflects most of the Sun's light rather than absorbing it.

Antarctic

The South Pole is located at a height of 2,836 m within the Antarctic Plateau. The ice is about 2,700 m thick at the South Pole. The coastal parts of Antarctica are slightly warmer than the interiors. The interior is a vast high plateau. It is colder because of its height, closeness to the South Pole and distance from the sea. The temperature stays around –20°C even in summer.

During winter, the size of Antarctica increases as the surrounding seawater freezes. There is very little precipitation. As a result, Antarctica is a desert.

 ISBN 978-81-8477-939-4

Circle Time

Icebergs are part of the landscape of the Frigid Zone. Find out what icebergs are and how they are formed. In what way are they dangerous? Share your findings in class.

Circle Time

Discuss the effects of global warming on the polar regions.

During summers, this region experiences natural displays of bright lights known as **auroras**. They are caused by the collision of charged particles in the Earth's atmosphere. The **Aurora Borealis** can be seen in the Northern Hemisphere, while the **Aurora Australis** can be seen in the Southern Hemisphere.

Factastic
The word 'Borealis' comes from the Greek name of the North Wind, Boreas, while 'Australis' means 'of the south' in Latin.

PLANT LIFE

Tundra

Very few plants are able to grow in the icy conditions of the Frigid Zone. In the North Frigid Zone, grasses, moss, lichen and some flowers grow in the short summer. The vast,

 ISBN 978-81-8477-939-4

treeless plains in the Arctic region are called the tundra. The permafrost does not allow trees to grow.

Moss

Lichen

WILDLIFE

Reindeer

Animals in the Frigid Zone have adapted to survive in the harsh climate. Many animals grow a thick coat of fur to keep warm. Some animals hibernate or go into a deep sleep in winter. They hibernate in underground burrows or pits. Some animals have a layer of fat to protect them from the cold.

Penguins

Animals such as Arctic fox, reindeer, musk-ox, polar bear, seal, whale, Arctic hare, Arctic wolf, snowy owl, snowy goose and walrus are found in the North Frigid Zone.

Animals found in the South Frigid Zone include penguin, albatross, Antarctic snow petrel, whale, seal, fish and squid. Some animals, such as the humpback whale, migrate to warmer waters at certain times in the year.

 ISBN 978-81-8477-939-4

Explore

Use an encyclopedia to find out five animals and five birds that have adapted to survive in the Frigid Zone.

People

The extreme cold conditions make most parts of the Frigid Zone uninhabitable. In the North Frigid Zone, some native people live a nomadic life. They include the Inuit in Alaska, the Lapps in Lapland and the Yakuts in north Asia. Many people depend on hunting for their survival. In some places, people have set up settlements. They earn a living from forestry, mining and tourism.

The native people have adapted to life on the frozen land. They build temporary houses such as igloos, out of blocks of ice. Some people live in tents. They hunt for whales, seals, walruses, fish and reindeer.

There are no permanent residents in Antarctica. Several countries have set up research centres where scientists live for short periods. Thousands of tourists visit Antarctica every year.

 ISBN 978-81-8477-939-4

Quiz Time

1. **Fill in the blanks to complete the following sentences.**

a. The Frigid Zone experiences long periods of __________ in summer and long periods of __________ in winter.

b. There are no __________ residents in Antarctica.

c. The coastal parts of Antarctica are slightly warmer than the __________.

d. The North Pole lies at sea level in the __________ Ocean.

e. The vast, treeless plains of land in the Arctic region are called the __________.

2. **Indicate whether the following statements are true (T) or false (F).**

a. Antarctica reflects most of the Sun's light rather than absorbing it. ☐

b. Very few plants are able to grow in the icy conditions of the Frigid Zone. ☐

c. The South Pole is located at a height of 2,836 m within the Antarctic Plateau. ☐

d. The North Pole lies at sea level in the Arctic Ocean. ☐

e. Large numbers of penguins are found in the Arctic region. ☐

 ISBN 978-81-8477-939-4

3. Draw lines to match the items listed in Column A with those in Column B.

	A			B
a.	Aurora Borealis	•	•	Lapland
b.	Aurora Australis	•	•	Northern Hemisphere
c.	Lapps	•	•	North Asia
d.	Inuit	•	•	Alaska
e.	Yakuts	•	•	Southern Hemisphere

4. Answer the following questions.

a. What is the latitudinal extent of the Frigid Zone?

b. Write a short note on Antarctica.

c. What is permafrost?

d. Why does the Frigid Zone experience a very cold climate throughout the year?

e. Write a short note on the flora and fauna of the Frigid Zone.

Why is there no permanent human settlement in Antarctica?

 ISBN 978-81-8477-939-4

9 INDIAN HERITAGE AND CULTURE

India has a diverse culture. Its culture includes all the knowledge and values shared by Indian society. India has a rich history in the various fields of music, dance, painting, sculpture and architecture. Indian culture is admired all over the world. Culture is passed on from one generation to the next. It forms India's heritage.

MONUMENTS

Monuments play an important role in telling the story of India's rich cultural heritage and history. Monuments were frequently built to mark an important occasion or event in history. Over time, they became important symbols of different periods of history.

QUTAB MINAR

The Qutab Minar is a red sandstone tower in Delhi. It is 72.5 m tall. It was built in 1193 by Qutab-ud-din Aibak, the first Muslim ruler of Delhi.

Qutab Minar, New Delhi

 ISBN 978-81-8477-939-4

The tower has five storeys and balconies. Its diameter measures about 15 m at the base and 2.5 m at the top. The first three storeys are made of red sandstone. The fourth and fifth storeys are made of marble and sandstone. At the foot of the tower is a mosque. There is a 7 m tall iron pillar in the courtyard of the mosque.

Humayun's Tomb

Humayun's Tomb is a creation that shows a blend of Persian architecture and Indian traditions. Built in the sixteenth century, the tomb is a square structure in red sandstone and is a World Heritage Site.

Humayun's Tomb, New Delhi

Fatehpur Sikri

Built in the sixteenth century by Emperor Akbar, Fatehpur Sikri (the City of Victory) is a complex of monuments and temples. It also contains one of the largest mosques in India, the Jami Masjid.

Fatehpur Sikri Complex, Fatehpur Sikri

 ISBN 978-81-8477-939-4

PARLIAMENT HOUSE

The Parliament House in New Delhi opened in 1927. It is a circular structure and has 144 pillars and broad corridors. The world's largest democracy functions from this building.

Parliament House, New Delhi

Khajuraho Temple, Khajuraho

Shore Temple, Mahabalipuram

The diversity of religious monuments shows the tradition of religious tolerance in India. There are churches, gurudwaras, temples and mosques all across the country.

St. Paul's Cathedral, Kolkata

 ISBN 978-81-8477-939-4

Major Monuments in India

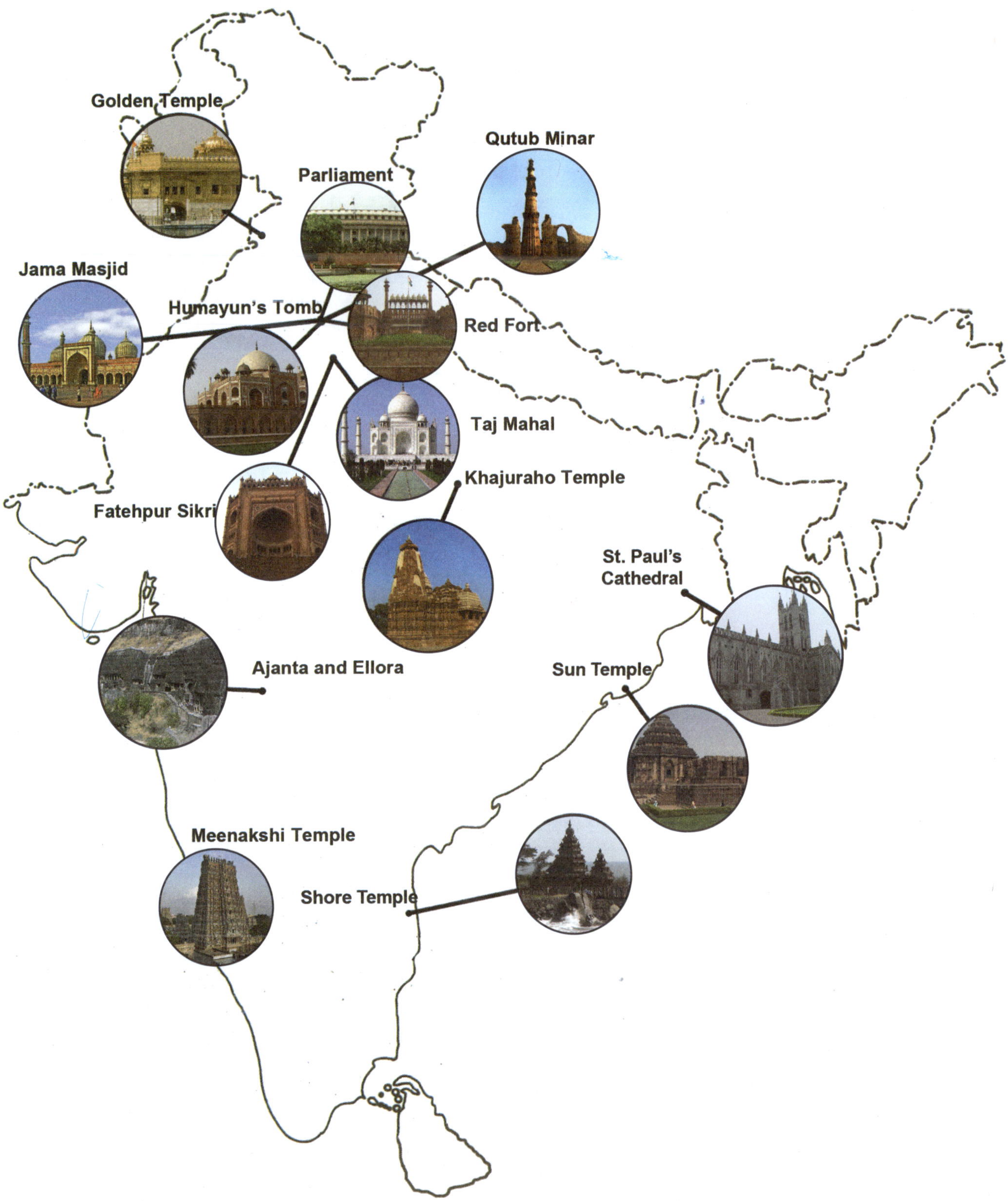

 ISBN 978-81-8477-939-4

Sun Temple

The Sun Temple, Konark

The Sun Temple, situated in the eastern state of Odisha, is constructed as a chariot with seven horses (symbolising the seven days of the week) and twelve pairs of wheels (symbolising the twelve months of the year), which carry the Sun god, Surya, across the heavens. The temple was built by King Narasimhadev (1238–1264 CE) of the Eastern Ganga Dynasty to celebrate a military victory.

UNESCO has declared this temple a World Heritage Site.

Explore

What is a World Heritage Site? Look up the Internet for information. List ten monuments that are World Heritage Sites.

Taj Mahal

Taj Mahal, Agra

Built on the banks of River Yamuna, the Taj Mahal was constructed between 1631 and 1653. A World Heritage Site today, it was built by Shah Jahan in the loving

 ISBN 978-81-8477-939-4

memory of his wife, Mumtaz Mahal. This white marble wonder has a central dome that is 73 m high. The structure combines the Persian, Indian, Islamic and Turkish styles of architecture.

Explore

The Taj Mahal is counted as one of the Seven Wonders of the World. Use the Internet or reference books and find out the names and locations of the other six.

Agra Fort

The construction of the Agra Fort started in 1565 under Akbar and was completed by his grandson, Shah Jahan. The fort is a unique blend of Central Asian and Hindu styles of architecture. Within the fort is the Moti Masjid, a white marble mosque. The Agra Fort includes the following structures: the Diwan-e-Aam, the Diwan-e-Khas, Khas Mahal, the Palace of Mirrors, the Pearl Mosque, the Nagina Masjid, the Garden of Grapes and the Fish Pavilion.

Agra Fort

Factastic

The Diwan-e-Aam used to house the famous Peacock Throne, which was taken to the Red Fort when Shah Jahan moved his capital to Delhi. The throne alcove is made of richly decorated white marble.

ISBN 978-81-8477-939-4

RED FORT

Red Fort

Also known as the Lal Quila, the Red Fort was built by the Mughal Emperor Shah Jahan when he transferred his capital from Agra to Delhi. It is made of red stone, from which it derives its name. The Red Fort was built between 1638 and 1648. It had fourteen gates, some of which have been demolished. The Mori, Lahori, Ajmeri, Turkman, Kashmiri and Delhi gates still exist.

Learn More

What is the present-day significance of the Red Fort?

JAMA MASJID

Jama Masjid

The Jama Masjid is situated across the road from the Red Fort in Delhi. It was built by Shah Jahan in 1656. The Jama Masjid means the Friday mosque.

Factastic

One of the oldest mosques in India, the Jama Masjid was built at a cost of ₹ 1 million. Its architect, Ustad Khalil, designed it to fit the entire population of the city. It is estimated that approximately 25,000 people can offer prayers at the Jama Masjid at one time.

 ISBN 978-81-8477-939-4

Meenakshi Temple

Meenakshi Temple, Madurai

The city of Madurai in Tamil Nadu is built around the Meenakshi Sundareshwar Temple. The temple was built by the Nayak Dynasty in the sixteenth century and is dedicated to Goddess Meenakshi. It is one of the greatest Shiva temples in India. The temple architecture draws inspiration from the Dravidian era, with richly carved pillars as well as *gopurams* (enormous gateways) and *mandapams* (halls with many pillars).

> **Factastic**
> The 'Chithirai' festival is held in April–May, when the celestial marriage of Meenakshi (goddess Parvati) and Sundareshwar (an incarnation of Parvati's husband, Shiva) is celebrated. This celebration draws crowds from all over the country.

The Golden Temple

The Golden Temple, Amritsar

The Golden Temple or the Harmandir Sahib was built in the lifetime of Guru Ram Das, the fourth guru of the Sikh community. It is surrounded by the Amrit Sarovar (Pool of Nectar), which is regarded as a sacred tank.

It was in 1802 that Maharaja Ranjit Singh gilded the roof of the temple. A white marble bridge leads to the temple. The entrances on all four sides signify that the temple is open to all.

 ISBN 978-81-8477-939-4

Sanchi Stupa

Sanchi Stupa

The Sanchi stupas are located north of Bhopal in the state of Madhya Pradesh. Ashoka, the Mauryan emperor, set up a Buddhist monastery and religious centre in Sanchi. Stupas are large semicircular domes containing a central chamber in which the relics of the Buddha were placed.

Gateway of India

Gateway of India, Mumbai

The Gateway of India overlooks the Arabian Sea. It was designed by the architect George Wittet to commemorate the visit of King George V and Queen Mary to India in 1911.

The architect combined the popular Indo-Saracenic style with the British, Mughal and Rajput styles of architecture. It was inaugurated on 4 December 1924 by the Viceroy, the Earl of Reading.

Factastic

The Gateway of India was the symbol of welcome that anyone sailing into Bombay Harbour first spotted. But after independence, it became a gesture of farewell as the last British regiment made its final exit from India from this very point.

 ISBN 978-81-8477-939-4

Learn More

Make a project on any historically important monument in India not discussed in this lesson, such as Victoria Memorial, the Mandu Fort, the Cellular Jail or the St Francis Church in Kochi.

Find out when this monument was built, where it is located and its significance. You can make your project in the form of a chart, a file or a computer display.

PAINTINGS

Cave painting at Ajanta

Indian paintings are diverse, historic and unique. They represent the cultural heritage and diversity that India is famous for.

These can be seen in the murals or wall paintings of the Ajanta and Ellora caves (in Maharashtra), the miniature paintings of Kangra and the Buddhist palm-leaf manuscripts.

The rock shelters of Bhimbetka, in Madhya Pradesh, saw the earliest drawings of huge figures of animals and humans, group dances and musical instruments. These paintings were made by rubbing colour on the rocks, using fingertips, twigs, brushes, or by spraying colour on the rocks using the mouth.

Rock paintings in Bhimbetka, Madhya Pradesh

 ISBN 978-81-8477-939-4

The caves of Ajanta have well-preserved wall paintings and sculptures providing a detailed description of Buddha's life and traditions. To paint these murals, the rock surface was first roughened so it could hold the plaster made of clay, lime, hay, dung and other natural materials. The colours and brushes were also made from natural materials.

Sculpture of Buddha at Ellora, Maharashtra

The fine sculptures of Shiva, Parvati and deities from the Mahabharata decorate the entrance and main temple of the Ellora Caves. The ceilings and walls are covered with bright colours.

Some traditional forms of Indian paintings are shown below.

Pattacchitra

Rajasthani

Warli

Mughal

Madhubani

 ISBN 978-81-8477-939-4

LITERATURE

Much before the invention of paper, Indians used to write on palm leaves with reed pens. A lot of literature was pictorial. Vedic literature comprising the four Vedas, the two great epics, Ramayana and Mahabharata, Panchatantra, Hitopadesa, Jataka Tales and Kalidasa's play *Abhigyan Shakuntalam* are important works of Indian literature.

CRAFT

The earliest examples of Indian craft date back to the Indus Valley Civilisation. Metal work, woodcraft, ivory carvings, pottery and textiles are only some of the forms of crafts found in India.

Quiz Time

1. **Draw lines to match the monuments listed in Column A with their location listed in Column B.**

	A	B
a.	Golden Temple •	• Madurai
b.	Humayun's Tomb •	• Mumbai
c.	Meenakshi Temple •	• Amritsar
d.	Gateway of India •	• Konark
e.	Sun Temple •	• New Delhi

 ISBN 978-81-8477-939-4

2. Indicate whether the following statements are true (T) or false (F).

a. The Sanchi stupas are located south of Bhopal in the state of Madhya Pradesh. ☐

b. The Golden Temple or the Harmandir Sahib was built in the lifetime of Guru Ram Das. ☐

c. The caves of Ajanta have well-preserved wall paintings and sculptures providing a detailed description of Mahavira's life and traditions. ☐

d. The Red Fort was built by the Mughal Emperor Shah Jahan. ☐

e. The construction of the Agra Fort was completed by Akbar's grandson, Aurangzeb. ☐

3. On a physical map of India, mark the location of the following monuments.

a. The Sun Temple

b. The Agra Fort

c. The Taj Mahal

d. The Ajanta Caves

e. The Golden Temple

4. Answer the questions.

a. What is the historical significance of the Taj Mahal?

b. What is the significance of the Sanchi Stupa?

c. What is the significance of the Sun Temple at Konark?

How are paintings important in the study of the past?

 ISBN 978-81-8477-939-4

10

THE ADVENT OF THE BRITISH RAJ

During the fifteenth and sixteenth centuries, some countries in Europe became very rich and powerful. They began exploring other parts of the world. They set up colonies around the world.

The first Europeans to come to India by sea were from Portugal. Portuguese explorer Vasco da Gama landed at Calicut (Kozhikode) in 1498. Portuguese spice traders set up trading centres at Cochin (Kochi), Cannanore (Kannur) and Calicut.

Vasco da Gama

In time, British, French and Dutch traders also arrived on Indian shores. They began trading Indian goods such as spices, silk, cotton, pearls and gold.

The Union Jack, the British flag

Over the next few years, the British became the most successful traders. In 1600, they set up the East India Company. They set up trading centres in many places including Bombay (Mumbai), Calcutta (Kolkata)

 ISBN 978-81-8477-939-4

and Madras (Chennai). The British built forts and started keeping their own army.

Factastic

As the East India Company gained popularity, the French set up their own trading company in Chandannagar (in Bengal) and Pondicherry (now Puducherry) near Chennai. But in a clash with the British, the French were forced to retreat and were allowed to retain only Pondicherry.

After the death of Mughal Emperor Aurangzeb, the Mughal Empire in India had become weak. The British took advantage of this and began to take over control. They captured many small kingdoms. By the middle of the nineteenth century, most of India was under British rule.

Learn More

On a physical map of the world, trace the route taken by Vasco da Gama to reach India.

Battle of Plassey

The Battle of Plassey marked the start of British domination over India. The battle took place at Plassey (Palashi), near Murshidabad, which was the capital of Bengal at that time. The French had their trading company in Chandanagore in Bengal.

Siraj-ud-Daulah

Siraj-ud-Daulah was the Nawab of Bengal. In June 1756, he captured the British trading base at Kolkata, Fort William. The East India Company

 ISBN 978-81-8477-939-4

sent its forces to recapture Calcutta. This led to the Battle of Plassey in 1757. The British army was led by Colonel Robert Clive and Admiral Charles Watson. The army had about 3,000 British and Indian soldiers. Siraj-ud-Daulah took the help of the French. His army had nearly 50,000 soldiers. But he was defeated, captured and put to death.

After the Battle of Plassey, the British became very powerful in Bengal. They took over Chandanagore from the French. They took a vast amount of wealth from the rich Bengal treasury. They used the wealth to strengthen their army. In 1764, the British won another battle, the Battle of Buxar. The East India Company took over control in Bengal.

The year 1757 is considered the start of British rule in India.

Explore

The Nawab of Bengal, Siraj-ud-Daulah had a much larger army than the British, but he was defeated. Research facts about the Battle of Plassey. Make notes and compile your findings in a battle report. Share your findings in class.

British Policies

Gradually, the British started conquering smaller Indian states. Many of these states were at war with each other. The British began to take advantage of this. They began friendly alliances with them. Later, they took control from their rulers. Two of these policies—the Subsidiary Alliance and the Doctrine of Lapse are discussed next.

 ISBN 978-81-8477-939-4

Learn More

Find information about any five Governor-Generals of India and the role they played in India. Present your findings as a chart, a file or a computer display.

Subsidiary Alliance System

Lord Richard Wellesley, the British Governor-General, used the Subsidiary Alliance system to bring many Indian states under British rule. According to the system, the British protected the states from threats, while gradually taking control over them. Some of the princely states that agreed to this alliance were Cochin, Jaipur, Hyderabad and Mysore.

Lord Wellesley

Under the terms of the policy of Subsidiary Alliance, the princely states had to disband their armies and allow British troops to maintain their states. As a result, the East India Company was able to maintain its army at the expense of the states.

Doctrine of Lapse

Lord Dalhousie introduced the Doctrine of Lapse to take over various Indian kingdoms. According to this policy, any kingdom would come under the direct control of the British if the ruler died without a direct heir.

Lord Dalhousie

 ISBN 978-81-8477-939-4

As a result of the Doctrine of Lapse, many Indian states came under British rule. They included Satara, Jaitpur, Sambalpur, Jhansi, Chota Udaipur and Nagpur.

Quiz Time

1. **Fill in the blanks to complete the following sentences.**

a. The ______________ were the first to establish their colony in India.

b. The Battle of Buxar was fought in ______________.

c. ______________ was the last Nawab of Bengal, who fought the battle of Plassey against the ______________ ______________ Company.

d. The year ______________ is considered the start of British rule in India.

e. The Governor-General of India, ______________, devised the Doctrine of Lapse.

2. **Write short notes on the following.**

a. The Doctrine of Lapse

b. Foreign merchants in India

c. The East India Company

d. The Subsidiary Alliance

 ISBN 978-81-8477-939-4

3. **Indicate whether the following statements are true (T) or false (F).**

a. The year 1757 is considered the start of British rule in India. ☐

b. After the Battle of Plassey, the French became very powerful in Bengal. ☐

c. The Mughals set up colonies around the world. ☐

d. The British took over Chandannagar from the French. ☐

e. Under the Doctrine of Lapse, the princely states had to disband their armies. ☐

4. **Answer the questions.**

a. Who discovered the sea route to India and when?

b. What was the impact of the advent of the British on the Mughal Empire in India?

c. What policies did the British use to gain control over various parts of India?

d. When and where was the Battle of Plassey fought? What was the main cause of the battle?

e. Which kingdoms were affected by the Doctrine of Lapse?

Why was the victory at the Battle of Plassey very significant for the British?

 ISBN 978-81-8477-939-4

11
The First Battle for Independence

The British continued to consolidate their control over India in the nineteenth century. The leaders and people of India began to rebel against the foreign power. They were unhappy at being treated unfairly in their own land.

There were various reasons that led to dissatisfaction among Indians. The British bought cotton at low prices from Indian farmers and exported it to Britain. Cotton mills in Britain manufactured cotton clothes, which were sent to India and sold at high prices. The British made huge profits through this two-way trade. As a result, the Indian handloom industry suffered terrible losses. Indian weavers were not allowed to start their own mills. Indian farmers were forced to grow crops, such as indigo, for which they were paid a pittance. The farmers thus struggled to earn a living. Over time, millions of people were driven to a life of poverty.

Besides, the British treated Indians as second-rate citizens in their own country. They took over the lands and properties of many Indian landowners. Many Indians were unhappy with the introduction of Western education and Christianity. Indian soldiers were paid poorly and treated unfairly.

 ISBN 978-81-8477-939-4

There were a number of revolts, but they were all suppressed by the strong British army. Then, a revolt in 1857 became a turning point in the history of India's freedom struggle. It became known as the Revolt of 1857 or the First Battle for Independence.

THE REVOLT

Bahadur Shah Zafar

The Indian revolt began on 9 May 1857 in Meerut. The British had introduced a new kind of rifle in the army—the Enfield rifle. The cover of the cartridges of these rifles was greased with animal fat. The soldiers had to bite off the cover before using the cartridge. The Indian soldiers believed that the cartridges were greased with cow or pig fat. Biting off the cover of the cartridge hurt the religious sentiments of both Hindu and Muslim soldiers.

Rani Lakshmibai

Mangal Pandey, an Indian soldier in the British army, rebelled against British officers. He refused to use the Enfield rifle. Other soldiers joined the revolt, too. This revolt soon spread across many places in north and central India. The most violent battles were fought in Delhi, Awadh, Rohilkhand, Bundelkhand, Allahabad, Agra and Meerut. In Kanpur, Nana Sahib was proclaimed the Peshwa

 ISBN 978-81-8477-939-4

by the rebel soldiers. Rani Lakshmibai was declared the ruler of Jhansi. She led her army to fight the British army. Bahadur Shah Zafar, the last Mughal emperor, was declared the Emperor of Delhi. The revolt continued for about a year.

Learn More

Find out the role played by Mangal Pandey in the uprising of 1857.

THE FAILURE OF THE REVOLT

The British were quick to suppress the revolt. They had an organised army and better weapons that helped crush the revolt. Many mutineers were tied to cannons and executed. The two sons of Bahadur Shah Zafar were killed. Rani Lakshmibai and Nana Sahib were both killed. The Mughal emperor was captured and sent into exile.

The revolt did not spread across the entire country. British rule was restored. In 1858, the territories of the East India Company in India came under the direct control of the British monarch. Queen Victoria was declared the Empress of India. The Queen appointed viceroys to govern India on her behalf.

Although the revolt failed to defeat the British, it became a turning point in India's history. The rule of the East India Company came to an end. The revolt inspired a feeling of nationalism among Indians. This grew into a larger movement for freedom.

 ISBN 978-81-8477-939-4

Circle Time

The British Empire was popularly described in the nineteenth century as 'this vast empire on which the sun never sets'. Study a map of the extent of the British Empire in the nineteenth century and have a class discussion on what was meant by this description of the British Empire.

Learn More

On a political map of India, mark the main centres of the Revolt of 1857.

THE INDIAN NATIONAL CONGRESS

In 1885, the Indian National Congress (INC) was formed. It provided the Indian people a platform to voice their opinion and draw attention to the problems that affected them. It brought

Lala Lajpat Rai
Lion of Punjab

Dadabhai Naoroji
The Grand Old Man of India

Bal Gangadhar Tilak
Father of Indian Unrest

 ISBN 978-81-8477-939-4

together people from different parts of India. Prominent thinkers and social reformers, such as Bal Gangadhar Tilak, Dadabhai Naoroji, Gopal Krishna Gokhale and Lala Lajpat Rai, were part of the INC.

The first session of the INC was held in 1885. W.C. Bonnerjee was the first president of the party. The INC was initially not against British rule in India. It made requests to the British Government to stop unfair trade, promote Indian industries and give Indians administrative rights. They believed that in time their demands would be accepted.

With time, some members became unhappy with the moderate ways of the INC. They wanted to take stronger action against the British to ensure that their demands were met. Leaders such as Bal Gangadhar Tilak, Bipin Chandra Pal and Lala Lajpat Rai wanted to take extremist ways.

In 1907, the party was divided into two groups: the *Garam Dal* (extremists) of Bal Gangadhar Tilak and the *Naram Dal* (moderates) of Gopal Krishna Gokhale.

Over time, the INC became a revolutionary party. It led the movement for freedom from British rule.

THE PARTITION OF BENGAL

Lord Curzon

The British Government tried to suppress the Indian demand for freedom. It tried to weaken the movement with a divide and rule policy. It decided that the Bengal province was too large to be managed properly. In 1905, the Viceroy of India, Lord Curzon,

ISBN 978-81-8477-939-4

divided Bengal into two parts—east and west. West Bengal, Orissa (now Odisha) and Bihar were on one side and east Bengal and Assam were on the other. East Bengal had a largely Muslim population while West Bengal had a largely Hindu population.

There were protests against the partition of Bengal in many parts of India. The INC also opposed the partition. The partition led to more anti-British protests across the country. It was followed by the formation of the All-India Muslim League and All-India Hindu Mahasabha.

Factastic

In order to bridge the growing divide between Hindus and Muslims and provide a platform for Muslim concerns, Salimullah Khan founded the Muslim League in Dhaka (the capital of Bangladesh). In 1913, Mohammad Ali Jinnah and Aga Khan joined the Muslim League.

The Swadeshi Movement

The Swadeshi Movement started soon after the partition of Bengal and continued up to 1908. Initiated by Gandhiji, the movement encouraged people to boycott British products and use only Indian or swadeshi goods.

Jamshedji Tata
Father of Indian industry

British products, such as clothes, were burnt in heaps as an open revolt. It became a mass movement. It spread from Bengal to other parts of the country. The main leaders behind the movement were Aurobindo Ghosh, Veer Savarkar, Bal Gangadhar Tilak, Bipin Chandra Pal and Lala Lajpat Rai.

 ISBN 978-81-8477-939-4

The movement helped revive local industries and production. It saw the growth of many domestic industries. A steel plant was set up by Jamshedji Tata.

Renowned scientist and nationalist, Dr Acharya Prafulla Chandra Ray established Bengal Chemicals & Pharmaceuticals Ltd. (BCPL), popularly known as Bengal Chemicals, in Kolkata.

The Swadeshi Movement forced the British Government to bring about some changes. In 1911, the British decided to reunite east and west Bengal. But, by then, the freedom struggle had become a mass movement. Revolts and demonstrations continued all across India.

Explore

Make a list of fifty objects that you use in your daily routine. Find out where these products are made. Are Indian products at par with imported or foreign-made goods?

Learn More

Make a project on any one leader of the Revolt of 1857. Highlight the contribution made by this leader to the revolt.

 ISBN 978-81-8477-939-4

Quiz Time

1. **Indicate whether the following statements are true (T) or false (F).**

a. Over time, the Indian National Congress became a revolutionary party. ☐

b. In 1858, the territories of the East India Company came under the direct control of the British monarch. ☐

c. The Revolt of 1857 inspired a feeling of nationalism among Indians. ☐

d. The Swadeshi Movement harmed local industries and production. ☐

e. In 1858, Queen Victoria was declared the Empress of India. ☐

2. **Fill in the blanks to complete the sentences.**

a. The Partition of Bengal took place in ________.

b. The Indian National Congress was founded in _____.

c. The first session of the Congress was held in _________.

d. Due to resentment, the eastern and western parts of Bengal were reunited in _____.

3. **Write short notes on the following.**

a. The Enfield rifle controversy

b. The Sepoy Mutiny

c. The Extremist faction of the Indian National Congress

 ISBN 978-81-8477-939-4

d. The Moderate faction of the Indian National Congress

e. The Swadeshi Movement

4. Answer the questions.

a. What were the causes for unrest amongst the Indians against British domination?

b. What was the uprising of 1857? How did the revolt serve as a turning point in the history of Indian independence?

c. What was the outcome of the Revolt of 1857?

d. What led to the division of Bengal?

Do you think a Swadeshi Movement would work to India's advantage today?

 ISBN 978-81-8477-939-4

12

The Struggle towards Complete Independence

Mahatma Gandhi

Mahatma Gandhi

Mohandas Karamchand Gandhi is regarded as the father of the Indian freedom struggle. He became one of the most respected leaders of the world. He is known as 'Mahatma' (great soul) for his values and contribution to India's freedom struggle.

Mahatma Gandhi was born on 2 October 1869 at Porbandar, Gujarat. He studied law in London and went to South Africa to practise it. At the time, the British ruled South Africa. Indians in South Africa were treated unfairly. Gandhi spent several years in South Africa working to fight discrimination. He created the idea of satyagraha, a non-violent way of protesting against injustice.

In 1915, Gandhi returned to India and joined the Indian National Congress (INC). He introduced satyagraha as a way to protest against British injustices.

 ISBN 978-81-8477-939-4

Rowlatt Act

In 1919, the British Government passed the Rowlatt Act. The Act gave the government the power to arrest and imprison people without a trial. The Act led to widespread protests. The INC called for a *hartal* or strike. It urged people to stop all business with the government and suspend work. Public meetings and protests were organised in many parts of the country.

The protests took a tragic turn on 13 April 1919 in Amritsar, Punjab. Public meetings had been banned in Amritsar. But a peaceful crowd of about 20,000 people had collected at Jallianwala Bagh, a walled garden that had just one exit. The British military commander, Brigadier-General Reginald Dyer, ordered his soldiers to block the exit and open fire. The firing lasted for about 10 minutes. Hundreds of people were killed and many more were wounded.

A memorial now stands at the site of the Jallianwala Bagh massacre site.

The massacre shocked Indians all over the country. The movement for freedom from the British became even stronger.

Factastic

The Rowlatt Act came to be known as the 'Black Act' as this Act gave the British Government the power to stop the newspapers from reporting and printing news.

ISBN 978-81-8477-939-4

Non-cooperation Movement

The Non-cooperation Movement was led by Mahatma Gandhi in 1920. People were asked not to cooperate with the British Government. Students and teachers left schools and colleges run by the British. Lawyers boycotted courts. Many people quit their government jobs. Some people surrendered titles and posts given to them by the British. People decided to buy only swadeshi goods and clothes. It was a peaceful nationwide movement.

Factastic

Rabindranath Tagore, noted poet, novelist, educator and an advocate of independence for India, returned the knighthood bestowed on him by the British Raj in 1915 as a mark of protest against the Jallianwala Bagh massacre.

Charkha used by Gandhiji

At times, the British tried to suppress the movement using force. Mahatma Gandhi stayed firm on non-violence. He motivated people to protest peacefully.

However, the Non-cooperation Movement turned violent at Chauri Chaura, Uttar Pradesh in 1922. People burnt down a police station and 22 policemen were killed in the incident. Mahatma Gandhi withdrew the movement. He was arrested on 10 March 1922 and sent to prison.

Bhagat Singh

 ISBN 978-81-8477-939-4

Many Indian leaders continued to protest against British rule. Revolutionaries such as Bhagat Singh, Chandrashekhar Azad and Bipin Chandra Pal have become martyrs in this struggle.

Bipin Chandra Pal

Chandrashekhar Azad

Learn More

Find information on Pandit Jawaharlal Nehru and his contribution towards the freedom struggle.

Simon Commission

In 1928, the British Government invited Sir John Simon to look into constitutional matters and to bring about reforms under the British regime. The INC boycotted the Commission because there were no Indians amongst its seven members.

People raised black flags in protest against the Simon Commission. Lala Lajpat Rai, an INC leader, was grievously injured when the British lathi-charged the protesters. He later succumbed to his injuries. His death further angered Indians and they continued the struggle with greater resolve.

 ISBN 978-81-8477-939-4

Mahatma Gandhi led the Civil Disobedience Movement in 1930. The aim of this movement was a complete disobedience of the orders of the British Government.

Circle Time

Discuss the significance of black flags.

THE CIVIL DISOBEDIENCE MOVEMENT

Mahatma Gandhi conducted the Dandi Salt March in 1930 and broke the Salt Law of the British Government. According to the Salt Law, Indians were not allowed to make salt from sea water. The British had total control over the manufacture of salt in India. Indians had to pay a high tax on salt.

On 12 March 1930, Mahatma Gandhi started his march from Sabarmati Ashram to Dandi on the shores of the Arabian Sea. Gandhi and a group of 78 satyagrahis walked about 380 km from Sabarmati to Dandi. They broke the Salt Law by making salt on the shores of Dandi. Many Indians were inspired by the Dandi March.

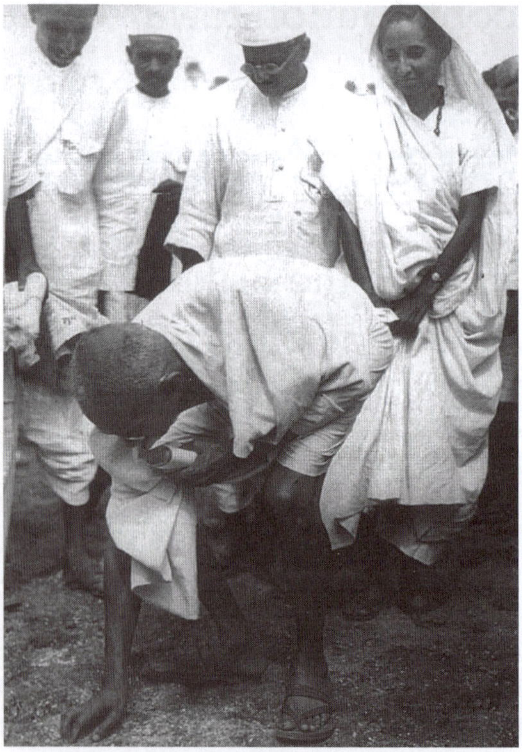

Gandhiji breaking the Salt Law in Dandi

The British tried to suppress the Civil Disobedience Movement by arresting people. More than 60,000 people were imprisoned. But more

 ISBN 978-81-8477-939-4

and more people continued to join the movement. They picketed shops selling foreign goods, refused to pay taxes and stopped attending work at public offices. The British imprisoned Mahatma Gandhi and Jawaharlal Nehru to suppress the movement. But the movement had widespread support across India.

Factastic

Gandhiji founded the Sabarmati Ashram on the outskirts of Ahmedabad. It is also known as the Satyagrah Ashram, Gandhi Ashram or Harijan Ashram.

Quit India Movement

On 8 August 1942, the Congress passed a strong resolution known as 'Quit India' Resolution (*Bharat Chhodo Andolan*). Mahatma Gandhi asked the British to quit India. He asked Indians to 'do or die' for their country.

Procession at Bangalore during the Quit India Movement

On 9 August 1942, Mahatma Gandhi was arrested. The other leaders continued the movement. The British tried to suppress the movement but were unsuccessful. India came many steps closer to achieving independence.

The Indian National Army

The Indian National Army (INA), also called the Azad Hind Fauj, was formed by Subhash Chandra Bose during World War II. Its slogan was *Delhi chalo*. The mission of the army was to wipe out the British rule from India. The Malayan campaign, the Burma campaign and the battles of Imphal and Kohima were

 ISBN 978-81-8477-939-4

fought by the INA in southeast Asia with the assistance of the Japanese.

Subhash Chandra Bose

The Azad Hind Fauj also had a women's unit. Although the INA came to an end within a short span of time, its role in the independence struggle of India is remarkable.

Circle Time

Have a class debate on the topic 'Peaceful protests are more effective than violent uprisings'.

Learn More

On a political map of India, mark the following cities: Porbandar, Amritsar, Chauri Chaura, Dandi and Kohima.

INDIA GAINS INDEPENDENCE

In 1945, the British finally decided to withdraw from India. On 15 August 1947, India became a free country. Pandit Jawaharlal Nehru became independent India's first Prime Minister and Dr Rajendra Prasad became the first President.

The British had created many differences between Hindus and Muslims as part of their divide and rule policy. This led to the partition of India into India and Pakistan.

 ISBN 978-81-8477-939-4

Quiz Time

1. Fill in the blanks to complete the following sentences.

a. Gandhiji started the historic Dandi March on the ____________.

b. The most significant phases in the struggle for independence were ____________.

c. Gandhiji was born on ____________. He was popularly known as 'Bapu'. Gandhiji's given name was ____________ ____________ Gandhi.

d. The Rowlatt Act was passed in ____________.

e. The British Brigadier-General ____________ was responsible for the death of hundreds at the Jallianwala Bagh.

2. Draw lines to match the events listed in Column A with the year in which they took place listed in Column B.

	A	B
a.	Quit India Movement •	• 1947
b.	Dandi March •	• 1919
c.	Jallianwala Bagh massacre •	• 1930
d.	Chauri Chaura •	• 1942
e.	Independence •	• 1922

3. Write short notes on the following.

a. The Jallianwala Bagh massacre

b. The Salt March

 ISBN 978-81-8477-939-4

c. The Azad Hind Fauj

d. The Quit India Movement

e. The Simon Commission

4. Answer the questions.

a. What initiated the Gandhian era in the struggle for independence?

b. Why did Gandhiji call off the Non-cooperation Movement?

c. What was the Rowlatt Act? What were its implications?

d. What was the Chauri Chaura incident? What was its result?

The Jallianwala Bagh tragedy was a turning point in India's struggle for freedom. Explain.

 ISBN 978-81-8477-939-4

13
Our Leaders

Several great leaders were part of India's freedom struggle. Their valuable contribution was instrumental in obtaining freedom. Some of these leaders are discussed next.

Rani Lakshmibai

Rani Lakshmibai
Icon of the Indian nationalist movement

Rani Lakshmibai of Jhansi was born on 19 November 1835 at Kashi (Varanasi) to Moropanth and Bhagirathibai. She was named Manikarnika. She married Gangadhar Rao, the Maharaja of Jhansi, in 1842. She studied self-defence, horsemanship and archery. She became the Rani of Jhansi and was given the name Lakshmibai. Gangadhar Rao did not have a natural heir and adopted Damodar Rao as his son.

The Raja of Jhansi died in 1853. As per Hindu tradition, Damodar Rao was the legal heir to the throne. However, the British refused to accept him as the legal heir. Following the terms of the Doctrine of Lapse, the British decided to seize the state of Jhansi. Rani Lakshmibai was firm about protecting the

 ISBN 978-81-8477-939-4

state of Jhansi and refused to allow the British to get control of her kingdom. She formed a volunteer army. She encouraged women to join the army and train to fight.

In 1858, the British attacked Jhansi. Rani Lakshmibai fought them bravely. The war went on for two weeks. Lakshmibai was joined by Tatya Tope and Nana Sahib. However, Jhansi fell to British forces. Rani Lakshmibai managed to escape with her son, but she was badly injured. She died in 1858.

Rani Lakshmibai became a symbol of courage. Her story inspired several Indian freedom fighters to rebel against British rule.

Factastic

Rani Lakshmibai was a symbol of courage for the people of India. She proved to be such a formidable enemy that the British offered a reward of Rs 20,000 for her capture.

Bal Gangadhar Tilak

Bal Gangadhar Tilak

Bal Gangadhar Tilak was born on 23 July 1856 in Ratnagiri, Maharashtra. He was a scholar of Indian history, Sanskrit, Hinduism, mathematics and astronomy. He was against Western education because he felt it did not respect Indian culture and values.

Tilak organised the Deccan Education Society to educate the youth. He brought out two weekly newspapers, *Kesari* in Marathi and *The Maratha* in English. The newspapers promoted the idea of patriotism and became very popular with the people.

 ISBN 978-81-8477-939-4

Tilak joined the Indian National Congress in the 1890s. In 1907, the Congress Party split into the *Garam Dal*, an extreme wing. Tilak led the wing along with nationalists Bipin Chandra Pal in Bengal and Lala Lajpat Rai in Punjab. They demanded complete independence for India. Tilak raised the slogan 'Swaraj is my birthright, and I shall have it!'

Tilak also helped found the All India Home Rule League in 1916–18 with Annie Besant and Mohammad Ali Jinnah. He appealed to people to boycott foreign goods. This led to a nationwide movement called swadeshi. It inspired patriotism among the people.

Tilak is regarded the father of Hindu nationalism. He was honoured with the title Lokmanya (beloved of the people). He died on 1 August 1920.

Vallabhbhai Patel

Vallabhbhai Patel

Vallabhbhai Patel was born on 31 October 1875 in Nadiad, Gujarat. His father, Zaveribhai, was in the army of Rani Lakshmibai of Jhansi.

Patel completed his high school education at Petlad and in 1910 went to England to study law. He returned to India three years later and started practising at Ahmedabad. Eventually, he gave up his practice to participate in the freedom struggle.

Sardar Vallabhbhai Patel, as he was later known, was deeply influenced by Gandhiji. In 1917, when Gandhiji was elected

ISBN 978-81-8477-939-4

the president of the Gujarat Sabha, Vallabhbhai was elected the secretary.

In 1918, Patel organised the peasants of Kheda and Borsad in a non-violent civil disobedience against oppressive policies imposed by the British Raj. He did the same in Bardoli in 1928. In 1930, Patel participated in the Salt March. He delivered inspirational speeches, encouraging people to join the satyagraha. In 1942, he joined the Quit India Movement.

In 1947, Patel became the first Deputy Prime Minister and Home Minister of independent India. He played a prominent part in the unification of India. He was able to convince a majority of the princely states to become part of the Indian Union.

Patel reorganised the Civil Services. He founded the Indian Administrative Service, Indian Police Service, Indian Foreign Service and other government services.

He was also known as the Iron Man of India. He died in 1950.

Sarojini Naidu

Sarojini Naidu
Nightingale of India
(*Bharat Kokila*)

Sarojini Naidu was born on 13 February 1879 in Hyderabad to Aghornath Chattopadhyaya and Varada Sundari Devi. Her father, a linguist, scientist and philosopher, founded Nizam College in Hyderabad. Her mother was a poet. Sarojini studied at the King's College, London and later at Girton College, Cambridge. She married Dr Govindarajulu Naidu.

 ISBN 978-81-8477-939-4

Sarojini Naidu was one of the most prominent leaders of the Congress and worked very closely with Gandhiji during India's freedom struggle. She was determined to bring about Hindu-Muslim unity and hence tried to unite the INC and the Muslim League. She was arrested in 1930 and in 1942. After independence, she was appointed the Governor of the United Provinces, now Uttar Pradesh.

Sarojini Naidu was a poet and spoke many languages. Some of her important works are *The Golden Threshold*, *The Bird of Time*, *The Broken Wing*, *The Feather of Dawn*, *The Feast of Youth* and *The Magic Tree*.

Sarojini Naidu was called *Bharat Kokila*—the Nightingale of India.

Factastic

Sarojini Naidu died on 2 March 1949 in her office at the age of seventy. Her birthday is celebrated in India as Women's Day.

Subhash Chandra Bose

Subhash Chandra Bose

Subhash Chandra Bose was born on 23 January 1897 to an affluent Bengali family in Cuttack, Odisha. He was a brilliant student who studied at Ravenshaw Collegiate School and graduated from Scottish Church College, Kolkata. He was strongly influenced by Swami Vivekananda's teachings and was also known for his patriotic enthusiasm. Although he had no intention of serving the British, he went to England to appear for the Indian Civil Service (ICS) examination only to please his father. He later resigned and joined the nationalist movement.

 ISBN 978-81-8477-939-4

Also known as Netaji, Subhash Chandra Bose was a fierce freedom fighter. He was elected the president of the INC in 1938 and 1939.

However, he did not agree with the views of other leaders in the party. He formed the Forward Bloc in 1939. He was jailed several times for his anti-British remarks and activities.

In 1941, he went to Japan and formed the Indian National Army (Azad Hind Fauj). He inspired his army with the words '*Dilli Chalo*'. With the words, 'Give me blood, and I shall give you freedom' he motivated people to join him in the fight against British rule. The army reached India on 18 March 1944 but it could not defeat the British forces.

It is believed that Netaji died in an aircrash on 17 August 1945. He is remembered for his patriotic spirit and his words—Jai Hind.

Explore

A sobriquet is a nickname. Bharat Kokila, Lokmanya, Iron Man of India are a few examples. Look up an encyclopedia or the Internet and find out the sobriquets of any five important personalities or countries.

Circle Time

Discuss how life would be if India was still under British rule.

Learn More

Make a chart on any Indian leader. Provide details about his/her life and accomplishments.

 ISBN 978-81-8477-939-4

Quiz Time

1. **Fill in the blanks to complete the following sentences.**

a. __________ brought out two weekly newspapers that inspired patriotism.

b. __________ was responsible for inspiring women to join the freedom movement.

c. __________'s army reached India on 18 March 1944.

d. __________ became the first Deputy Prime Minister and Home Minister of independent India.

e. Sarojini Naidu was appointed the Governor of __________ after independence.

2. **Indicate whether the following statements are true (T) or false (F).**

a. Sarojini Naidu was honoured with the title Lokmanya. ☐

b. Subhash Chandra Bose went to Japan and formed the Indian National Army. ☐

c. Bal Gangadhar Tilak raised the slogan, 'Swaraj is my birthright, and I shall have it!' ☐

d. Rani Lakshmibai formed a volunteer army but discouraged women to join it. ☐

e. Vallabhbhai Patel studied law in England. ☐

 ISBN 978-81-8477-939-4

3. Draw lines to match the leaders listed in Column A with their birthdays listed in Column B.

	A	B
a.	Rani Lakshmibai •	• 13 February 1879
b.	Bal Gangadhar Tilak •	• 31 October 1875
c.	Vallabhbhai Patel •	• 23 January 1897
d.	Sarojini Naidu •	• 23 July 1856
e.	Subhash Chandra Bose •	• 19 November 1835

4. Answer the questions.

a. Who is known as the 'Iron Man of India' and why?

b. Whose famous words were 'Swaraj is my birthright, and I shall have it!'? What was his contribution to the struggle for freedom?

c. What was the Azad Hind Fauj?

d. How did Rani Lakshmibai become a symbol of courage?

e. What was the Doctrine of Lapse? How did it affect Rani Lakshmibai?

Why do you think Subhash Chandra Bose did not agree with the views of the other leaders of the INC?

 ISBN 978-81-8477-939-4

14

Religious and Social Reformers

For a country to prosper, the ideas and beliefs of the people have to evolve with the changing times. Here we discuss some of the people who devoted their lives to bring about social and religious changes for the betterment of our society.

Raja Ram Mohan Roy

Raja Ram Mohan Roy

Raja Ram Mohan Roy was born in 1772 to a rich family of Bengal. He studied various languages including Persian, Arabic, Sanskrit and English. He published his first book *Tohfat-ul-Mohiddin* in 1803 in which he stated that all religions preached the worship of one god. He strongly criticised idol worship and meaningless religious rituals.

Raja Ram Mohan Roy worked as a religious and social reformer. He was against the barriers of caste divisions and social evils, such as sati, and propagated widow remarriage. The British Government abolished sati in 1829 largely in response to Roy's campaign against this practice.

sati: an old practice of burning widows alive along with the body of their dead husbands on the funeral pyre
propagate: to spread and promote an idea or theory widely

 ISBN 978-81-8477-939-4

He wanted Indian society to move away from superstitious rituals to a more rational worldview. He condemned the unfair treatment meted out to peasants by the zamindars. He started the Brahmo Samaj in an attempt to change the excessive dependence on religious rituals in society. He demanded that women be given the right of inheritance and property.

Raja Ram Mohan Roy had very liberal views on education for girls and hence opened various schools for them.

He is regarded as the Father of the Indian Renaissance.

Circle Time

Find out more about the tradition of sati. Discuss what changes you would like to see in society.

Sir Syed Ahmad Khan

Sir Syed Ahmad Khan was born in 1817 in Delhi. He was an Indian educator and politician who pioneered modern education for the Muslim community in India. He wrote a booklet after the war of independence of 1857 on the causes of the mutiny. Sir Syed strongly blamed the

Sir Syed Ahmad Khan

superstitious: to believe in the irrational fear of what is unknown or mysterious, especially in connection with religion
condemned: to judge or pronounce to be unfit for use or service; to pronounce to be guilty; sentenced to punishment
liberal: favourable to progress or reform in political or religious affairs
pioneered: to take part in the beginnings of; initiate; to lead the way for (a group); guide

 ISBN 978-81-8477-939-4

British and their unfair policies for the revolt. Sir Syed organised relief for the famine-struck people of the Northwest Frontier Province in 1860. He established a modern school in Ghazipur and a madrasa in Muradabad, which was the first of its kind to impart scientific education. He also founded the Muhammedan Anglo-Oriental College, which later became the Aligarh Muslim University.

Swami Dayanand Saraswati

Swami Dayanand Saraswati

Dayanand Saraswati was born in Tankara, Gujarat, to a wealthy Brahmin family. He was named Moolashankar and was also called Dayaram. He was one of the most important socio-religious reformers in India.

Swami Dayanand Saraswati founded the Arya Samaj or the Society of Nobles in Mumbai in 1875. He was a scholar and believed in the authority of the Vedas. He also established *gurukuls* to impart Vedic education. He strongly disapproved rituals such as idol-worship, the caste system, untouchability, child marriages and animal sacrifices. He believed that salvation was attainable only through service to society.

He worked towards equal rights for women and their right to education. He translated the Vedas from Sanskrit to Hindi to make them easy for all to read.

madrasa: a school attached to a mosque where Islamic instruction is imparted

 ISBN 978-81-8477-939-4

Swami Dayanand was one of the first to introduce the concept of swaraj. He founded the Dayanand Anglo Vedic schools all over north India with the aim to spread knowledge and education.

Learn More

Compare the ideas and beliefs of Raja Ram Mohan Roy with those of Dayanand Saraswati.

Pandita Ramabai

Pandita Ramabai

Pandita Ramabai was born in 1858. Her father, Pandit Anantshastri Dongre, a great scholar, defied society and taught Sanskrit to his wife, Lakshmibai Dongre, and two daughters. Ramabai laid the foundation of the women's liberation movement in India. She addressed several public meetings where she spoke against gambling, drinking and other evil habits that destroyed families. She encouraged widow remarriage.

Ramabai established Sharda Sadan, a home for widows and poor and needy women. Ramabai wanted women to be self-confident and independent. She founded the Arya Mahila Samaj and the Poona Seva Sadan which offered vocational training to women.

defied: challenged the power of; resisted boldly or openly
vocational training: training for a specific occupation or employment

 ISBN 978-81-8477-939-4

The Pandita Ramabai Mukti Mission is still active today. It provides housing, education, vocational training and medical services to widows, orphans and the blind.

VINOBA BHAVE

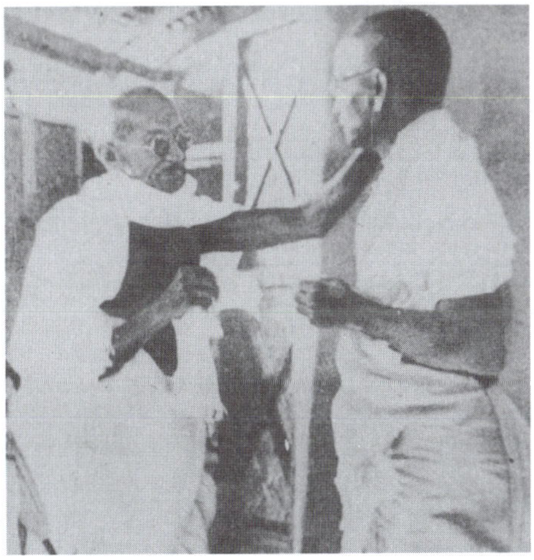

Vinoba Bhave with Gandhiji

Vinoba Bhave was born on 11 September 1895 in the village of Gagoda, Maharashtra. His real name was Vinayak.

He was a spiritual **visionary** and became a symbol for the struggle of 'good against evil' and for the spiritual against the ordinary. He gave up his high school studies in 1916 and became an enthusiastic follower of Gandhiji. He led a rigorous life, dedicated to improving the life of Indian villagers.

Bhave was jailed several times between 1920 and1930 for his anti-government activities. He was an active participant in the non-violent struggle against the British Raj for which he served a five-year prison sentence in the 1940s. He was given the title of *acharya* (teacher). He was a social reformer and founded the 'Bhudan Yajna' or the land-gift movement in 1951. He appealed to rich landowners to donate land to landless Untouchables or Harijans.

In 1958, Vinoba Bhave became the first recipient of the international Ramon Magsaysay Award for Community Leadership. He was also awarded the Bharat Ratna, India's highest civilian award, in 1983.

visionary: a person who thinks or plans the future with imagination or wisdom

 ISBN 978-81-8477-939-4

Frank Anthony

Frank Anthony

Frank Anthony was born on 25 September 1908 in Jabalpore, Madhya Pradesh. An intelligent student, he studied at Nagpur University where he excelled in English and was awarded the Viceroy's gold medal. He later moved to London and obtained a degree in law.

Frank Anthony returned to India and started practising law. He was against the partition of India because he felt it would affect the minority communities in India.

Factastic

The All India Anglo-Indian Educational Trust presently runs five public and junior schools in Kolkata, Delhi and Bengaluru named after Frank Anthony.

He represented India in the Commonwealth Parliamentary Conference in 1948 and 1957. He was also part of the first delegation of independent India to the United Nations.

Frank Anthony contributed towards the spread of education by establishing the All India Anglo-Indian Educational Trust. He was appointed the chairman of the Inter-State Board of Anglo-Indian Education.

Frank Anthony wrote the book *Britain's Betrayal in India: The Story of the Anglo-Indian Community*. He died in 1993.

 ISBN 978-81-8477-939-4

Explore

Find out about any one Indian social or religious reformer not discussed in this lesson. Note down the details of his/her contribution to Indian society and present your findings in class. You can make your presentation as a booklet, a chart or a computer display.

Quiz Time

1. Indicate whether the following statements are true (T) or false (F).

a. Vinoba Bhave was awarded the Bharat Ratna. ☐

b. Frank Anthony helped establish special provisions for the Anglo-Indians in the Constitution. ☐

c. Pandita Ramabai supported sati and purdah. ☐

d. Sir Syed Ahmad Khan encouraged modern education among the Muslim community in India. ☐

e. Ram Mohan Roy was born in 1774. ☐

2. Fill in the blanks to complete the following sentences.

a. ______________ formed the Brahmo Samaj to bring about social and religious changes in the society.

b. ______________ appealed to rich landowners to donate land to landless people.

c. ______________ was given the title of *acharya*.

ISBN 978-81-8477-939-4

d. ____________ supported freedom for women and protection of widows and child brides.

e. The British Government passed a law abolishing sati in ____________.

3. Draw lines to match the social and religious reformers listed in Column A with the institutions they founded listed in Column B.

	A			B
a.	Raja Ram Mohan Roy	•	•	Arya Samaj
b.	Sir Syed Ahmad Khan	•	•	Arya Mahila Samaj
c.	Swami Dayanand Saraswati	•	•	Brahmo Samaj
d.	Vinoba Bhave	•	•	Aligarh Muslim University
e.	Pandita Ramabai	•	•	Bhudan Movement

4. Answer the questions.

a. Why was sati abolished?

b. Who established the Sharda Sadan?

c. What was the Bhudan Movement?

d. Who is regarded as the Father of Indian Renaissance?

e. Why did Swami Dayanand Saraswati establish the Dayanand Anglo Vedic schools?

All social and religious reformers in India spoke in favour of the spread of education. Why?

ISBN 978-81-8477-939-4

15
Our Rights and Duties

The Constitution

The Lion Capital of Sarnath

India is a democracy with a parliamentary system of government. It follows the laws and principles laid out in the Constitution. The Constitution was adopted by the Constituent Assembly on 26 November 1949. It came into effect on 26 January 1950.

The Constitution of India is the supreme law of the land. It defines the country's political values. It defines the structure, procedures, powers and duties of the government. It also outlines the rights and duties of India's citizens.

Factastic
Republic Day is celebrated on 26 January each year. It was on this day, in the year 1950, that the Union of India was declared to be a sovereign, democratic republic.

Learn More

Imagine you are the Prime Minister and your class is the country you govern. Make a list of rules and regulations for your 'country' keeping in mind the best interests of all the 'citizens'.

 ISBN 978-81-8477-939-4

Fundamental Rights

The Constitution provides all citizens some basic freedoms. They are called Fundamental Rights. The Fundamental Rights ensure that all citizens can live in a free and democratic environment. These rights are guaranteed in the Constitution. The Supreme Court of India and State High Courts have the power to enforce the Fundamental Rights.

There are **seven** categories of Fundamental Rights.

Right to Equality

The Right to Equality is the right of every citizen to be treated equally. All citizens have equal privileges and opportunities. This Fundamental Right protects citizens against discrimination on the basis of caste, race, sex, place of birth and religion.

Right to Freedom

The Right to Freedom guarantees all citizens the right to think and express themselves freely. Citizens have the right to assemble peacefully. They may form associations or unions. All citizens have the right to live and travel freely within the country. All citizens also have the right to join any profession or choose any occupation or business.

Cultural and Educational Rights

All citizens of India have the right to follow their own culture, customs, traditions, script and language. They have the right to establish and administer educational institutions of their choice.

Right to Freedom of Religion

Every citizen has the right to choose and practise the religion of his or her choice.

 ISBN 978-81-8477-939-4

Right against Exploitation

This right protects the citizens of the country against any kind of exploitation, forced labour, slavery, begging and human trafficking. This right protects children against child labour. No child under the age of fourteen can be employed.

Right to Constitutional Remedies

Every citizen of the country is allowed to stand up in defense of his or her rights, even against the Indian Government. Citizens can take their grievances to court, right up to the level of the Supreme Court, the highest protector of law in India.

Right to Education

The Right of Children to Free and Compulsory Education Act or the Right to Education Act (RTE) came into force on 1 April 2010. This Act makes education a fundamental right of every child between the ages of 6 and 14 and specifies minimum norms in elementary schools. It requires all private schools to reserve 25 per cent of seats for children from poor families.

Circle Time

Imagine a society without any rules and regulations, without any law and order! Discuss with the class the advantages as well as disadvantages (if any) of having laws.

human trafficking: transportation, harbouring or receipt of people for the purposes of slavery or forced labour
grievances: a wrong considered as grounds for complaints, or something believed to cause distress; a complaint or resentment, as against an unjust or unfair act

 ISBN 978-81-8477-939-4

Fundamental Duties

There are certain Fundamental Duties that citizens of India are bound by. As citizens of India, we are morally bound to perform the following **Fundamental Duties**:

- To respect the Constitution of India, all government institutions and laws, national symbols, the national flag and the national anthem.
- To respect and cherish the freedom struggle and all those who helped India attain independence.
- To defend the country and to be ready to provide national service if the need arises.
- To always encourage and promote the feeling of unity and brotherhood.
- To renounce derogatory practices such as dowry.
- To cherish and preserve our rich cultural heritage, natural environment and resources.
- To protect and preserve public property.
- To work towards excellence in all areas so that the country can rise to higher levels of achievement.

Directive Principles of State Policy

The Constitution lays down certain principles for the government to follow. They are called the Directive Principles of State Policy. It is the duty of the government to apply these

derogatory: tending to lessen the merit or reputation of a person or thing

 ISBN 978-81-8477-939-4

when it makes laws. They are guidelines for creating a fair and just society.

Some Directive Principles of State Policy are:

- To promote social, economic and political equality.
- To provide equal opportunities to means of livelihood.
- To provide early childhood care and education for all children until the age of 14 years.
- To raise the standard of education and health.
- To protect historical monuments.
- To promote international peace and security.
- To maintain just and honourable relations with other nations.

Quiz Time

1. Fill in the blanks to complete the following sentences.

a. The ____________ lays down the structure, procedures, powers of the government of India.

b. Republic Day is celebrated on ____________ each year.

c. The Union of India was declared to be a sovereign, democratic republic in the year ____________.

d. The Constitution provides the citizens of India with ____________ Fundamental Rights.

e. The Right ____________ protects citizens of the country against any kind of exploitation, forced labour, slavery, begging and human trafficking.

 ISBN 978-81-8477-939-4

2. **Indicate whether the following statements are true (T) or false (F).**

a. Every Indian has six Fundamental Rights. ☐

b. India became a republic in 1947. ☐

c. The Constitution came into effect on 26 November 1949. ☐

d. We are not morally bound to defend the country and to be ready to provide national service if the need arises. ☐

e. The right to form associations and unions is granted to all Indian citizens as part of the Right to Freedom. ☐

3. **Answer the questions.**

a. What is the Constitution of India? When did it come into existence?

b. What are Fundamental Rights?

c. What are Fundamental Duties?

d. What are the Directive Principles of State Policy?

'Fundamental Rights and Fundamental Duties are two sides of the same coin'. Explain.

 ISBN 978-81-8477-939-4

16
The United Nations

Following World War I (1914–1918), a need was felt for an international organisation that would help maintain world peace and order. It was with this aim in view that the League of Nations was formed in 1919.

The League of Nations comprised forty-two countries and worked to maintain coordination and cooperation between countries in order to allow for economic and social progress.

However, when World War II (1939–1945) broke out, it was realised that the League had failed in its objectives. Without any military support of its own, the League had not been successful in maintaining world peace.

In 1944, representatives of China, the United Kingdom (UK), the United States (US) and the Soviet Union (USSR) met in Washington, DC, to lay down the foundation for an international organisation.

On 26 June 1945, fifty-one countries signed the Charter of the United Nations (UN). The Charter came into force on 24 October 1945. Presently, the UN has 193 member states.

Factastic

Although Poland was unable to send a representative to the San Francisco conference when the UN Charter was being drafted, it is nonetheless considered an original member of the United Nations (UN). India joined the UN on 30 October 1945.

 ISBN 978-81-8477-939-4

The UN came into existence with the aim of bringing all the nations of the world together to work towards global peace and development. It finds its roots in the principles of justice, human self-respect and the welfare and security of all.

The UN emblem

The UN emblem is the world enclosed in the olive branches of peace.

The UN encourages its member countries to keep aside individual interests and focus on global issues that affect all nations.

It functions like an individual country with a separate government. There are six major bodies that function within the UN:

- The General Assembly
- The Security Council
- The Economic and Social Council
- The Trusteeship Council
- The International Court of Justice
- The Secretariat

The members meet in the **General Assembly** to weigh world opinions. Each country is entitled to a single vote to be cast during times of decision-making. Being the most important part of the UN, the **Security Council** is responsible for international peace and security. In times of conflict, in any part of the world, the Security

Seal of the International Court of Justice

 ISBN 978-81-8477-939-4

Council conducts peace talks to maintain harmony. It sends peace-keeping forces to places affected by wars.

> **Factastic**
> Dr Nagendra Singh of India was the president of the International Court of Justice between 1985 and 1988.

The Economic and Social Council manages problems that are related to issues such as famine, drought, poverty and illiteracy.

The **International Court of Justice** settles legal disputes submitted by the member states.

The **Secretariat** maintains records and files of the meetings held by the UN. The head of the UN Secretariat is the **Secretary-General**.

> **Factastic**
> The UN headquarters is in New York City (USA); but the land on which it stands and the buildings it occupies are considered international territory. The European headquarters is in Switzerland. Other offices are in Vienna and Austria. The UN Economic Commissions are in Addis Ababa in Ethiopia, Amman in Jordan, Bangkok in Thailand and Santiago in Chile.

The UN has its own flag, post office as well as postage stamps. It has six official languages: Arabic, Chinese, English, French, Russian and Spanish.

The UN aims to develop and maintain cordial relations between member countries. It advocates peace throughout the world. The primary aim of the UN is to help eliminate disease, poverty and illiteracy from the world. It encourages nations to protect and preserve the environment. It also urges nations to work together with mutual respect for each other's rights.

cordial: courteous and gracious; friendly; warm
advocate: to speak or write in favour of; support or urge by argument; recommend publicly

The UN and its member states work on the following principles:

- All member states must obey the Charter.
- All member states must respect each other's independence and authority.
- All disagreements between the member states shall be sorted by peaceful methods, without the use of force.
- The member states shall support the UN in all its activities.

The UN has several specialised agencies, such as the United Nations International Children's Emergency Fund (UNICEF), the World Health Organisation (WHO), the United Nations Educational, Scientific and Cultural Organisation (UNESCO), which work with the UN as well as with each other.

These agencies are separate, independent intergovernmental organisations that work in fields like agriculture and development, communications and transport, humanitarian assistance to developing countries and so on. They depend on funds from member states to achieve their goals.

Learn More

Find out which of the specialised UN agencies operate in India. What projects have they undertaken?

The various member states of the UN observe a few universally celebrated festivals. These are discussed next.

intergovernmental: involving two or more governments or levels of governments

 ISBN 978-81-8477-939-4

World Health Day is celebrated on 7 April each year. Various events to promote good healthy living are held on this day.

International Earth Day, celebrated on 22 April each year, is a day to re-evaluate our responsibility towards our planet and the environment. On this day, we renew our pledge to take care of the Earth by planting new saplings.

International Labour Day (also known as May Day) is celebrated on 1 May every year. It is celebrated to honour all those who work in factories, workshops, industries and mills.

World Environment Day is celebrated on 5 June every year to create and spread more awareness about preserving the environment.

In the year 2007, the UN General Assembly decided to celebrate 2 October (Mahatma Gandhi's birthday) as **World Non-Violence Day**. This was done to commemorate Gandhiji's ideology of non-violence.

Circle Time

Work with your classmates to make a project titled 'One World—One Planet—One Home'.

 ISBN 978-81-8477-939-4

Quiz Time

1. Draw lines to match the international days listed in Column A with the dates on which they are observed listed in Column B.

	A		B
a.	World Health Day •		• 1 May
b.	International Earth Day •		• 2 October
c.	May Day •		• 22 April
d.	World Environment Day •		• 5 June
e.	World Non-violence Day •		• 7 April

2. Fill in the blanks to complete the following sentences.

a. The League of Nations was formed after World War __________ (1914–1918).

b. The League of Nations consisted of __________ countries.

c. By the end of the ____________, fifty-one countries signed the Charter of the United Nations. It was signed on ____________ 1945.

d. Presently, the membership of the UN has increased to ____________ member states.

e. ____________ is celebrated to commemorate Gandhiji's ideology of non-violence.

 ISBN 978-81-8477-939-4

3. Expand the following acronymns.

a. UNICEF

b. WHO

c. UNESCO

4. Answer the questions.

a. What was the purpose for the formation of the League of Nations?

b. When was the United Nations formed? What are its aims?

c. Who heads the Secretariat of the UN?

d. What are the specialised agencies of the UN? Name a few.

e. What are the main principles of the UN?

In your opinion, how far has the UN been effective in meeting its aims? Why?

 ISBN 978-81-8477-939-4

How to Use an Atlas

A collection of maps compiled into an easy-to-use format is called an atlas. An atlas is a widely used resource in any classroom. Maps help us to identify and locate places around the world, learn more about the settings of stories, understand the historical and newsworthy locations and even do distance calculations. Atlases may be general and cover the entire globe, or they may be specific to geographical locations, topics or time periods. An atlas can have maps detailing the physical and political features, tourist spots, climate, natural resources, land, sea and air routes.

All maps are reduced to fit the size of the page, according to a scale. The two main types of maps according to scale are:

Large scale maps, which show great details of a small area. For example, the map of a city.

Small scale maps, which provide general information of a large area. For example, the map of a country.

NORTH is depicted at the top of all maps. Most maps have a grid of lines, which helps to locate the place. Parallels are lines that represent distances north and south of the Equator. Meridians are lines representing east and west of the Prime Meridian.

An atlas usually has an index at the end of the book. The index is an alphabetical listing of place names and their pronunciations. It gives you longitude and latitude coordinates as well.

Suppose you have to locate INDORE. Look up place name in the index. It may be given as INDORE 13 D4. Go to page 13 and locate INDORE in the grid box D4.

For teachers

A. Display a large map in your classroom. Every morning when students come, write the 'Find Out' or a 'Question of the Day' related to the map.

Questions may include:

How many states border Maharashtra?

Through which states does the Ganga River flow?

In which part of the world is Kenya?

B. Ask the students to create a map of their neighbourhood or colony. Encourage them to use their own keys or symbols. It will be interesting to see what each student chooses as an icon for the legend.

Tips

- Use atlases that are up to date. States and countries sometimes change names and borders. For example, what was once Czechoslovakia (one country) is now Czech Republic and Slovakia (two countries). Similarly, if you are using a road atlas for directions, make sure it is a recent one.
- Study the key or symbol guide to the maps. Each atlas uses different symbols. Symbols are important to know what you are looking for on the maps.
- Use the table of contents to find maps for your research.

 ISBN 978-81-8477-939-4

How to Use an Encyclopedia

An encyclopedia is a useful resource found in all libraries. An encyclopedia may be a single volume, subject specific, or multi-volume covering a wide range of topics. Because encyclopedias are so easy to use and so accessible, many people use encyclopedias as their first option for a reference tool.

Most general encyclopedias are multivolume sets and are set up in alphabetical format. Some encyclopedias may need you to know the key word or subject heading in order to find specific information covered over a variety of volumes. Some encyclopedias devote separate volumes to different subjects.

Locate the index. The index is usually in the last series of volumes and is in alphabetical order. It gives you page numbers and volume numbers to locate the article you are researching.

Read the article and pick out relevant information for your project.

For teachers

A. Pass a volume of an encyclopedia to a group of students. Ask them to go through the layout, the way the information is organised and the quickest way to locate an entry. Challenge each group to compile an encyclopedia on any topic. Topics could be children's authors, unique inventions, historical sites in Asia, etc.

B. Ask the students to read an entry on any animal of their choice. Encourage the students to write a newspaper article or a poem using all the details and facts from the entry.

Tips

- Look out for other cross-references that can broaden your topic and provide new insight into your research.
- Pay attention to the maps, graphs and pictures in the article.
- The outline, provided for longer articles, is a helpful reference tool when organising your writing.
- Refer to authors correctly. The information on authors is either in the introductory material or in the index.

How to Use the Internet

One of the most recent and popular resources for research is the Internet. The Internet is a repository of information collected from various sources. Navigating through sites and links can give you updated information. Though the Internet is a wealth of information, before proceeding on any topic, take an adult's help to determine which sites might be reliable and which might not.

For teachers

Divide the class into four groups. Give three groups a topic to research. Each of these groups will have to research from different sources. The fourth group will then review the depth and breadth of the information collected by each, and survey and compare all the sources. It can base its report on:

Which source gave the maximum amount of information?

Which source gave the better information?

Tips

- It is a good idea to sit with an adult and bookmark the sites that you will need for research. This way you can directly go to the pages you want to view.
- Before beginning the topic, write down some keywords on which you will base your research.
- Use quality, child-friendly search engines, such as Ask Jeeves Kids (www.ajkids.com) and Yahooligans! (www.yahooligans.com). You can keep a list of helpful sites near the computer for easy access.
- Quotation marks are important while conducting a topic search. If you enter your topic or key words without quotation marks around it, the search will give information about anything linked to the words. If you put the search topic in quotation marks, you will get information related to the exact words placed within quotation marks.
- If you can't read through the entire article, you can use the FIND option to locate a particular word in the article.

 ISBN 978-81-8477-939-4